PARENTING
teenagers

CLAIRE SHORT

Scripture Union
207-209 Queensway, Bletchley, Milton Keynes, Buckinghamshire, MK2 2EB

Scripture Union, 207–209 Queensway, Bletchley, Milton Keynes, MK2 2EB, England.

First published 1996

ISBN 1 85999 031 2

British Library Cataloguing-in-Publication Data
A catalogue record for this book is available from the British Library.

Cover design by Ross Advertising & Design Limited.
Cover illustration by Taffy Davies.

Printed and bound in Great Britain by Cox & Wyman Ltd, Reading.

I dedicate this book to our two daughters,
Amanda and Carolyn,
who have taught Stan and me so much!

Contents

Preface

If you are one of those parents who claim to have blinked and missed the period of adolescence in your children, and wonder why every other parent cannot cope as you did – you have opened the wrong book! Please, however, bear with the rest of us and tolerate our feelings of inadequacy!

Not since they were under-5 has there been so much significant change in your son or daughter's life. The age of adolescence is an exciting one, with much to celebrate and enjoy; but it is also a time when many difficult issues emerge. Never before has so much pressure been put on young people by society; and society's expectations may far exceed youngsters' abilities, denting their confidence if not demolishing it altogether.

Most of the problems heaped at the door of adolescence are not exclusively those of the individual or of their parents but, rather, are concerned with how adolescents and parents manage the dynamics – what goes on between them – during this period. For this rite of passage does not just belong to the young person, but to his or her parents too. Sadly, casualties do happen in the parent-child relationship, but if this time is managed and negotiated successfully a mutually satisfying love and respect can emerge.

Like their children, parents need to grow and develop. This book will, I hope, address some of the lessons for adults during adolescence. As parents, we must discern the situations that cause problems between us and our children, so that we come to understand them a little better. We also have to recognise that we may never completely understand them! However, as you read these pages, you may find that you are enabled to clarify your role and to become more self-aware, to learn and grow, not just for your teenager's benefit but for your own development too. As your son or daughter stands poised on the brink of adulthood, now is the time to take stock and evaluate your part in helping them get there successfully – because there *is* life after adolescence, for you as well as your child!

This is a small book about a huge subject. I have not been asked to write it as a paragon of parental virtue but as one who has learnt by her mistakes. It does not cover every problem that a parent might encounter. However, I hope that some of your questions will be answered and that you will be on the way to sustaining a rewarding relationship with your son or daughter; this relationship could be their greatest resource in this time of transition.

Claire Short

Acknowledgements

Page 39: *Families and How to Survive Them*, John Cleese and Robin Skynner, Methuen (1983).

Pages 41 and 44: *Parent Effectiveness Training*, Dr Thomas Gordon, New American Library (1970).

Page 58: *The Gift of a Child*, Claire Short (ed), Stroud, Lion Publishing (1982).

All statistics throughout verified by OPCS (Office of Population and Census Surveys).

1

Recognising the signs

Imagine the scene. Toys and fluffy animals that were once inseparable from your offspring have been removed from their favourite place in the bedroom and are now in plastic bags awaiting transportation to the attic, charity shop or – even more drastically – the bin! Walls are covered in posters. Every surface is arrayed with an assortment of cans and bottles. If you are extremely lucky, you will detect a square inch of colour on the floor, suggesting that the carpet is alive and well under the ever-growing piles of clothes, papers, magazines and shoes. Adolescence has arrived!

Perhaps one of the most important things to grasp, when you are struggling with any particular stage of your child's development, is that it is experienced by the family as a whole and not just by an individual in isolation. Adolescence may be focused on one or more members within the family, but the behavioural side – or dynamics – affects the whole unit and determines how this stage is negotiated. Just as the young person is endeavouring to cope with the onslaught of physical and emotional change, parents or carers are also thrown into confusion. They have never been the parents of adolescents before. Everything is unfamiliar!

11

Recognising adolescence

It is difficult to pinpoint a time when adolescence begins. Each individual has – through their own personality, culture and environment – their own internal time clock. Throughout history, recognition of this time of life has been confused: teenagers were regarded either as children or as adults and did not behave appropriately for either category! It is only during the last fifty years that this social grouping has had its own identity and that we have begun to explore the behaviour patterns which accompany it. For the purpose of this book, I am suggesting that the adolescent stage covers approximately the early teenage years to age twenty, though many psychologists would extend this into early adulthood.

It wasn't that long ago that thirteen-year-olds were in full-time employment, and they still are in some parts of the world today. However, in Western society, formal education lasts longer and young people are dependent on their parents financially until they get a job or go on to university or college; yet the onset of puberty is happening earlier due to improved nutrition and health care. These factors, coupled with later marriages and longer life-expectancy generally, extend the period of adolescence and delay the time when the young person is finally able to become completely independent of his parents.

Parents' adjustment to change

One of the things that parents find hardest to accept in their adolescent is the young person's changing identity. The search for identity is what this stage of growing up is all about and, in order for it to stabilise in early adulthood, it first has to be disrupted. We are comfortable with the child who has emerged from being a toddler and started school. Behaviour and character is predictable and, although the child is changing and developing, the pace is manageable and parental authority still holds sway. This is the child who we know and love and can relate to with some degree of success.

The first inklings of change are often spotted by parents before their children are aware of them. Emotional mood swings accompany the physical development of puberty, and the two are linked by intensive hormonal activity and biological change. Puberty, with its growth spurts and altering bodily contours, heralds the fact that childhood is about to be left behind. According to individual personality, reactions to and acceptance of this are as varied as the shapes that emerge! Many a parent has tentatively suggested that a visit to the lingerie department of Marks and Spencer may not come amiss on observing T-shirts and blouses straining at the seams! On the other hand, your offspring may have a preoccupation with her figure that has you shopping around for a 28AA cup just so that she can keep up with her friends! Sons too can have an obsessive attachment to the tape measure and spend the next few years identifying with Adrian Mole, anxiously comparing themselves with their peers.

This often painful consciousness of self is characteristic of most children as they enter puberty, and a sensitive and wise response from parents is required. I well remember when our daughter brought home her first-ever bra. We realised that my husband's humorous comment of 'What does she want *that* for? She's got nothing to put in it!' had been overheard when a red, tearful face emerged and exclaimed, 'I'm preparing for the future!' We learnt a lot from that incident. As parents, we need to understand that how our children see their world is not necessarily how *we* see it. Unless we listen to them when they tell us how they understand their experiences, we cannot begin to be of any help to them during this critical period of development. (Fortunately our daughter has forgiven us!)

The transition to adulthood seems to promote more stress for the family than any previous stage. Why? The fact is that the question of identity is not only of concern to your teenager. As a parent, how comfortable are *you* with who you are? Are you secure and confident in most aspects of your personality? In all of us there is a vulnerable spot, an area of insecurity that surfaces under stress and anxiety. This may be related to feelings of rejection or inadequacy, not feeling special or loved, or the need to be the 'perfect' parent and get everything right – as if such a parent could ever exist!

Adolescence can seem to come at the most inconvenient time for parents. Just as our children have everything in front of them, we are becoming aware of the advancement of our own mid-life. The firmness of their young bodies confronts the predictable result of the force of gravity on our own! Parents' attitude to themselves will influence their attitude towards their children, and with all the issues that emerge in adolescence they too need to take time to make the journey inward. We must recognise the buttons that will be pressed by our son's or daughter's emerging sexuality. We must get to grips with the 'letting go' process. We must come to terms with the fact that our values will be challenged as they are re-assessed by our children in the here and now, and no longer adhered to mindlessly because they have always been around.

Discovering uniqueness

Much of my work is concerned with the area of personal development, and it is so rewarding to see people who have struggled for years with aspects of their personality, change, develop and be released into wholeness. It takes courage to face your real self and courage to change.

It is God who brings wholeness into humanity, but we through our fallibility make mistakes and fragment the wholeness he desires for each one of us. Many look to 'in' social trends or other people for affirmation and, in doing so, repress their own personalities. Christians too can sacrifice freedom in Christ to become pale 'clones' of each other.

However well-practised the performance, its limitations soon show. Each of us is a unique individual and, while we can learn good things from others, we cannot substitute our lives for theirs. Each family unit is unique too. Situations and characteristics may be similar, but they can never be the same as those of any other family!

We will never be perfect parents (not in this life any-way!). Situations may have arisen that we wish we had han-dled differently, or we may have treated our children in ways that we need to be forgiven for. The good news is that it is never too late to change! The greatest gift we can give our children is unconditional love – for them and for ourselves too, taking our model from our heavenly Father who loves and accepts us.

Early childhood themes revisited

A popular remark hurled at many a teenager is 'Stop acting like a five-year-old!' Although its delivery seldom elicits the desired response of 'Yes, OK then!', there is perhaps a grain of accuracy in this description of adolescent behaviour.

The 'terrible twos' is a stage that many a parent would like to draw a veil (or a nappy) over, and we now see it return with greater degrees of intensity! The years between two and five are an age of great energy and discovery – that's the 'up' side. But – and here comes the 'down' side – these years are a time when parental authority is tested and power struggles begin. The answer to the question 'Who's in charge around here?' seems to oscillate between the parent and the toddler: the former may deal effectively with a tantrum; the latter holds maximum power over both ends of their digestive sys-tem! Sounds familiar?

If you were able to retain your dignity then, hang on to it now because you are really going to need it! In adoles-cence all the themes of early childhood re-emerge. Issues of trust, dependency, social adaptation, control and authority are each taken up and worked through again, but this time with greater impact on and significance for those involved. The problem for parents is that they cannot and should not address these issues in the same way that they did in their child's infancy. Some do, and end up with total chaos! The issues of trust and dependency established during the first eighteen months of your baby's life are now part of your teenager's life too. Just as your son or daughter was totally dependent on you for food and security during the first months of life, so they are dependent on you being there now – to test out their independence and show that they can exist without you. The fact that they often can't is just one of the paradoxes characteristic of this stage.

A more detailed look at trust and dependency follows in a later chapter. For the moment, let us be aware that though your response to your adolescent's behaviour will be tested from all sides, it will be the foundation stone on which relationships are built for the future. If conflicts between you and your teenager are not resolved, they will invade your child's journey into adulthood in a way which causes far greater and longer lasting damage than did the battles between you and your two-year-old.

Power struggles

It seems a common scene in most families. Your teenager wants to go to X's party and stay the night. *Everybody* will be there and *their* parents are far more reasonable than you are! You say 'No', they say 'Yes' and, after much time and energy is spent, you are advised, as your son or daughter exits to their room, to 'Chill out and relax!'

The trouble is that while youngsters seem to thrive on these highly charged outbursts and have the energy for an action replay, you are left stressed out and exhausted. There was a time when your authority was accepted, albeit reluctantly; ultimately, *you* had the last word. Now your authority is questioned and challenged. So what are power struggles about and how can they be managed more effectively?

First, we cannot and should not try to eliminate them. Parents who practice dictatorship demanding absolute compliance are ensuring that their children always feel resentful towards authority figures and never learn to handle power responsibly. I have seen too many cases, sadly often in Christian families, where children are not allowed or encouraged to express opinions and feelings which are different from those of the rest of the family: they are punished or shouted down into resentful submission. It comes as no surprise to find that their behaviour becomes uncontained and socially unacceptable as a result, causing great distress to those involved. Power struggles can be bruising affairs for both sides. When we are confronted with a different view of life we often become amazingly defensive, and maintaining a superior position takes precedence over anything else. Many of these encounters could be avoided if parents took time to understand *why* an issue is so important to their children, and were prepared to learn from their perspective.

Amy's parents had always insisted that she dress according to their taste and values – neatly and conservatively. They were mortified when the 'black stage' came and Amy wanted to wear black jeans and tops like her friends. (I remember this stage well with my own teenagers – woe betide me if I washed a garment wrong and it came out grey!) In reality the choice of these new clothes was relatively harmless to Amy, but her parents' outrage and their need to keep Amy as they wanted her brought a great deal of hostility and rebellion which could have been avoided.

In our own family, my husband and I decided not to waste useless energy on small issues that didn't really matter too much. Instead, we saved it for the bigger ones where discipline and clear boundaries were necessary. Parents may lose the occasional battle, but once the limits are established a full scale war can be avoided!

2

Letting go

From the moment parents first hold their newborn infant in their arms, their task is to enable her to achieve independence and lead her own life. The ongoing process of separation, which starts with the cutting of the umbilical cord, is tested further when the child starts school, and is ideally realised when the young adult moves away from home to establish her own unit and take full responsibility for her life.

Some parents find, however, that 'letting go' is a manoeuvre fraught with problems. While the animal kingdom has no trouble pushing its offspring out of the nest, we humans seem reluctant to release our children into the adulthood that we have prepared them for. The cord may have been severed physically, but emotionally it can prove extremely hard to separate. The 'letting go' process has to be practised and rehearsed well before the young adult actually leaves, so that it is a natural part of development and not a sharp shock of rejection and emotional trauma.

A couple known to us were treating themselves to a long overdue weekend away, and were anticipating a relaxing and enjoyable time. I was therefore surprised to see Julie looking anxious on the morning before they were due to depart: 'It's the first time we've left our two on their own. I know they're old enough to be left but I can't stop worrying if they'll be OK – and Rob has just got this new girlfriend!' Such is the power of love *and* fear. I have no doubt that every parent goes through the same nagging thoughts. At what stage, we wonder, can we hand large responsibilities over to our children? I remember my own feelings when our daughter passed her driving test and went off that same evening in *my* car!

What then is happening in the adolescent 'arena', and how can parents balance the two conflicting concepts of 'holding on' and 'letting go' without constant battles with their offspring? The parental 'arena' too has much happening in it. It is by trying to understand the anxieties of both camps, that a way may be found to achieve some measure of harmony between them.

Dependency

First, let's consider what 'holding on' is all about, because it can mean different things to different parents. The majority see maintaining control of their children's behaviour as a way of protecting them from the world outside which is only too ready to take advantage of their impressionable youth. Protection is, of course, a worthy principle, appropriate and necessary for growing children. By adolescence, however, the gradual process of handing over responsibility should be well under way.

From early years, your son or daughter will have been used to receiving instructions and implementing them so as to demonstrate care and consideration for themselves and others; but as they get older there is more and more emphasis on their taking greater responsibility for their own behaviour. *You* may delight in ironing all your teenager's clothes (are there really people who enjoy ironing?) and may choose to continue to do it. Fine – but your son or daughter should know *how* to iron and to cook, and have all the basic skills they need to get through life independently. Learning to drive, for instance, means taking responsibility for a car. My husband and I took the view that if our teenagers were competent enough to drive a car, they were also able to clean it and fill it with petrol! We saw this as a way of introducing them to life in the real world and of acknowledging that we trusted them enough to behave like adults.

So often obsessive protection is confused with love. It isn't. It can be a totally selfish act by parents, stunting their children's emotional development and preventing them from coping in today's society. Even if you are comfortable financially, your children still need to learn how to budget, to wait for the things they want, and sometimes to do without. This is not withholding things from your children but equipping them for what they may face in adulthood, and it will store up valuable skills for life. The story is told about a son who kept giving his parking tickets to his parents. While they continually baled him out, he went on re-offending. But when they finally handed over responsibility for paying the parking fines to him, he stopped. He realised that he had to take responsibility for his own actions.

Of course, the teenager is for the most part financially dependent on his parents. The concept of reward for favours done is an area that parents may have different views on. The parent who 'rewards' her toddler for performing on the potty or putting all the toys away may need to think whether this kind of recognition is appropriate as the child gets older. The child may get the message that he need only take responsibility for chores when there is a reward such as pocket money or a treat. My own view is that pocket money should be given regularly, without conditions and not linked in any way to behaviour. Taking responsibility and helping out with certain family chores should be dealt with separately so as not to confuse love and giving with performance. Verbal rewards – spoken words of appreciation – are valuable and can be backed up with the occasional love-gift or present.

Taken to its extreme, the inability to let go can turn a

healthy desire to protect into a need to control and suppress any changes in the adolescent that we, as parents, are unprepared for. We must be willing to adjust and to examine our motives, but this may be uncomfortable! Rather than confront our own areas of inadequacy and anxiety, we can, almost by reflex, say 'No you can't' to every request we find difficult. There will, of course, be occasions when 'No' is necessary. But sometimes, when we are put on the spot by our children, we should take time to think. 'Give me a moment to mull it over' or 'I can't give you an answer immediately – come back in five minutes', often provides the space to assess the situation and your own response without jumping in and then having to back down on a hasty decision. Your child may feel impatient, but could actually be pleased that you have taken time to think things through.

So often parents' inner panic at not holding tight to the reins reinforces their need to control their children's behaviour and ambitions. A mother was heard to say recently that she had discouraged her son from going to university, even though he had the right grades and was anxious to go, because she didn't want college life to interfere with the family unit. By having him around at home, she would be protecting him from an 'unhealthy' environment and ensuring that he didn't change from the son she knew and loved. This is perhaps a sad example of the need to hold on outgrowing its effectiveness and becoming restrictive.

This brings us to the second aspect of 'letting go' – that of parental dependency. As parents, we need to check out how dependent *we* are on our children. Our assumption is that they are totally dependent on us and, of course, for most of their childhood this is true. But let's not deny the place that children play in our own dependency needs. If your offspring are the *sole* source of your identity, the only responsibility you have, the only channel through which you can assert your own personality, then you have trouble ahead. 'Letting go' will provoke feelings of fear and loss: without your children you will have lost your own identity; without the parenting role your sense of purpose evaporates and your life becomes empty. It is time for you to evaluate your talents and to seek outlets for them. If you neglect to do this, you may find yourself indulging in jaded, outmoded and inappropriate parenting which seeks to control the lives of your children with regard to their relationships, their marriages and their children, instead of finding fulfilment in your own.

While we may originally choose to have children to satisfy our own desires, they cannot be the sole source of our fulfilment: it is too heavy a burden and responsibility for them to bear.

Trust

It is perhaps in this emotive area of 'letting go' that trust needs mutually to be tested and proved. If we are Christian parents, we place our children in God's hands and trust him for their safety and protection, as it is right to do; but running alongside our prayers for them, there may be the feeling that God needs more of a helping hand from us than is really required! My mind goes back to an incident in our kitchen when I was anxiously repeating every piece of advice that we had given to our sixteen-year-old daughter regarding drugs, drink and sex. You name it, I saw it happening in graphic detail! The more my imagination was fed, the more panicky I felt. The more fearful I became, the faster I spoke as I endeavoured to cram every talk, book and piece of wisdom into five minutes! I was duly reminded, with a resigned smile, 'Mum, you and Dad have taught me all about this – you now have to *trust* me to put it into practice. You can't come everywhere with me and hold my hand!' Out of the mouths of babes, as they say!

There comes a point in every family when the parenting role finishes as a duty, and the need to guide your children comes to an end. The relationship – your love, your care and concern – will go on forever, but the responsibility for your young adult's life must be handed over to them. It is my own view that by the time youngsters have reached eighteen, parents have imparted all the teaching about life that they can. From that age onwards there are too many other sources of influence vying for your children's attention. It is rewarding and extremely precious when they ask for your opinions and advice, and value the comments you make. The decision, however, on whether or not to *take* that advice is theirs and theirs alone. Parents cannot and should not even attempt to impose it!

Among his many wise offerings the witty Mark Twain was reported to have said, 'When I was a boy of fourteen, my father was so ignorant I could hardly stand to have the old man around. But when I got to be twenty-one, I was astonished at how much he had learned in seven years.'

Such is the arrogance of youth!

A new audience

From an early age, your child has used you – the parent – as her primary audience. Strutting around the floor in your clothes or constructing unidentifiable objects out of the middles of toilet rolls and bits of plastic, you have been the one from whom she has sought approval. You may have responded favourably (or otherwise!) to what she did; you may have smiled delightedly at the paintings, models and other results of her creative endeavours at play-group or school, brought home with pride to show you. Now the curtain has come down on this scenario and a new audience is wooed – that of the peer group.

Friends are vitally important to your teenager, and they will prove to be the transition between the security of the family and that of a lasting relationship in adulthood. To be sure, friendships will always be of value and may even continue into adulthood. But, at this time as never before, their friends will have a prominent place in the adolescent's life.

Gone are the days when a family outing on Saturday was

a carrot to dangle in front of an unco-operative child! Gone are the days when family holidays were that all-fulfilling idyll, playing Monopoly while the rain poured down outside. Gone are the evenings in, when parents could rest in the knowledge that all was safe and well, with all the family under one roof!

Now holidays are times when everything is 'boring'. Saturdays are spent walking, without any specific purpose and no money, around the local shopping centre with friends; or playing sport, and then, in less time than it takes to ask 'What are you doing next?', rushing in, having a shower and disappearing out the front door again, munching a sandwich. Whenever the phone rings, it's *not* for you – it's their friends, with whom they have just spent all day but can still find loads to talk about which can't wait until tomorrow! And, when they're older, you spend your evenings wondering who they're with, what they're doing and where on earth *are* they anyway? Friends are taking over your territory. They influence your teenager's choice of clothes, the way he speaks and the music he listens to. Friends' approval is vital and held in high esteem. Parents seem to have become redundant.

However, parents still hold a prominent and important position in their offspring's life, and, by adapting to your child's changing needs, you are strengthening not weakening the ongoing relationship between you. Your child is the product of *your* parenting. Up till now *you* have moulded his personality, character and identity: his values will have been taken from yours, and his moral code and ethics constructed from the values you have. This then is the foundation, the launch pad from which your child takes off to establish his own value system and identity. If he has not been taught to behave in a socially acceptable way, to value and appreciate people and property around him, then it is not within his power suddenly to acquire these skills during the changing period of adolescence.

> Train a child in the way he should go,
> > and when he is old he will not turn from it.
> > > (Proverbs 22:6)

These verses present us with both a general principle to apply and a timeless challenge. Parents' responsibility is to train up their children so that they can handle all that life brings them. And the values parents give will always be remembered, even when they are not adhered to.

A new identity

Searching for and establishing an identity means that the adolescent has to separate himself from his parents, and determine which aspects of his personality have been acquired and which are his own. Inevitably, there will be differences. This search for self may be a source of confusion, and part of this process is that your teenager will endeavour to stick on parts of other people's identities that seem attractive to him – creating a sort of identikit personality. This may include aspects of others' mannerisms, dress, lifestyle, etc, and will go on changing until your teenager is comfortable with the person he is.

Eventually, your child should reach the point where he can acknowledge and fulfil his potential as the adult God planned him to be. This, of course, is the desirable goal. But I have to say that I know many people – parents too – who take on parts of other people's personalities and characteristics in order to feel whole and adequate themselves. There is a disturbing tendency in many churches today towards this type of 'cloning'. People look alike, dress alike and act in the same way; they seem insecure and lacking in the spiritual confidence that might have enabled them to develop as individuals with their own gifts and personalities. The joy of experiencing people coming to faith and joining a church can be undermined as they change from being colourful, unique individuals, each with his or her own opinions and mannerisms, into carbon copies of the people sitting either side of them! So often Christians feel that to become more 'spiritual' they have to take on not only the beliefs of the fellowship but the body language and fashions as well. That fresh individuality which celebrates the variety in humanity is now replaced by dull uniformity – greatly diminishing the impact of Christian witness to the world around.

Parents can model themselves on other families and wonder why, when they try to live up to what they see as ideal, it doesn't work for them. Kay was always trying to emulate the mother of her daughter's friend. The friend's mother dressed beautifully, had a pristine house and was the perfect cook and hostess. Trying to integrate this image into her own nearly brought Kay to a breakdown. Realising the stress she was putting on herself and her family, she abandoned the attempt and gave herself permission to be the person she really was. Her family were much happier and Kay a great deal more content.

In passing, I would like to comment briefly on the role of youth leaders and workers and the responsibility they have as 'significant adults' in the lives of young people in the church. Youth leaders can be looked up to and idealised, and what they say taken as law. The youngsters they work with will certainly be interested to see if they practise what they preach – they will be under scrutiny! As leaders, they will have to exhibit spiritual maturity and sensitivity, and conduct themselves in a way that offers no negative role model to follow.

The wrong identity

We have seen that teenagers identify with others in their sub-culture. The adolescent's inner world is chaotic and unreliable. By fixing on the outer world of groups, ideologies and images – whether it is the latest 'supermodel', 'soap' star or member of a band – he invests energy in reconstructing himself, taking ideas about himself from a variety of people and sources. This stage is harmless enough. It is as if the adolescent is using these people as a mirror to reflect how he would like to see himself. The problems come when he over-identifies with a group or individual who will turn out to be destructive.

Most parents would probably identify with the fear that their children will be involved with the 'wrong' kind of friends. This fear can be exacerbated by finding out that your son or daughter is getting involved in petty crime or taking on values that are unhelpful both to them and to society. These liaisons generally develop during the secondary phase of education and can seriously disrupt the child's learning process. The worst thing you can do, however, is to forbid your son or daughter to see the friends you disapprove of. This only serves to make them defensive and label you 'paranoid' and unaccepting. Better to show your concern in a way which doesn't put friends down or rubbish them as people, but which allows your child to see that you are anxious without resorting to panic measures. Even if it means gritting your teeth, invite their friends in, talk to them and try to discern where the area of unacceptance is. It will then be easier to communicate your worries to your teenager.

Hazards faced by Christian parents

There is always joy and thankfulness, and perhaps some self-satisfaction, when your teenager accompanies you of his own free will to church. A Christian family is a wonderful heritage. You may find, however, that there are certain hurdles to be crossed when your child reaches adolescence.

The first may be that of coming to faith. Being brought up in a Christian environment may mean that faith is a part of one's culture and tradition, which is no bad thing. But there needs to be a clear understanding of what is the parental faith and what is the youngster's own. Separating these two strands may lead to much searching and questioning on the part of the individual, and this can rock the boat in the Christian home. Schools will teach theory as fact and, as like as not, pour scorn on Christian commitment. Your son or daughter will face serious challenges to their Christian beliefs and, because they will be in the minority, may feel vulnerable and exposed. Don't over-react or squash them if they question truths that have been part of your established teaching for years. Instead, pray for them, listen to them and try to understand the necessity for this questioning process. If your children eventually do come to a relationship with God, it will be more meaningful and precious because it has stood the test of such investigation. It is so good to see young adults in our churches who have thought their faith through and who can communicate it to others.

Being known by a church from early childhood has its down side. While Christian parents may accept (with grace or otherwise!) the changes in their teenagers, others in the church may not be so accommodating. 'Whatever has happened to nice little Amy? She used to be so cheerful and polite. Now she looks so shabby in those awful jeans and army boots, and she always seems so bored!' This kind of comment can set even the most gracious parent's teeth on edge. But then not everybody will understand the changing moods and behaviour which are becoming familiar to you.

There is usually constant pressure on the children of church leaders, with much expected of them and an almost perverse curiosity in their failures. These may come to be branded *your* failures. I remember well one Sunday evening – it was Mother's Day – when our fifteen-year-old was *supposed* to be at the evening service with her friends. I was at home with the younger one, preparing refreshments for the meeting after the service in the manse which adjoins the church. A police van pulled up outside with some young people in it, including an extremely sheepish daughter. Nothing serious had occurred, just some pranks on bikes, and as part of the group she had been gathered up with the others. The police had no sooner departed than the church

29

folk began to file into the house as I verbally challenged (it sounds better than 'yelled at'!) my daughter on the doorstep. My parting shot as she rushed upstairs was 'Nice one... Perfect timing... Happy Mother's Day to you too!'

Church leader's children have a lot to cope with. Without any choice in the matter, they are in the same gold-fish bowl as their parents. They may hear criticism of their parents from others who forget momentarily who they are, and this has left many a child of the manse or vicarage disillusioned, hurt and angry. In addition, the accusation of 'You shouldn't do that, you're the minister's/vicar's son/daughter' should be banned from the lips of church members. The minister's offspring are individuals independent of the roles of their parents.

Leaving the 'home' church to try another one is a path that some, not all, teenagers may need to tread in order to grow and mature in their own right. This step is an act of independence, and it is important that parents do not regard it as rejection of the church but rather as an exploration within it. Often new-found confidence manifests itself as a young person finds her gifts and uses them without the pressure of parents witnessing her every move and mistake.

Youngsters in the church youth group may also feel pressurised to conform to certain standards by other church members. The church may be worried by the low numbers of young people, and the few teenagers who do come may feel the weight of expectation from adults to be the perfect witnesses to others in their peer group. Yet they too need the freedom to express themselves so that they grow and mature in the faith. While it feels good to have a consistent and familiar youth group as part of the church, we need to allow it to be a living organism which changes shape and size in order to develop and fulfil its potential in the body of Christ.

Perhaps the most distressing experience for Christian parents is when their children fall away and reject the teaching they have passed on to them. When your teenager declares that she doesn't want to come to church anymore, don't plunge instantly into the depths of despair! Try to establish first *why* this decision has been made. The reasons may range from the popular 'Because it's boring' to 'My friends laugh at me', 'Sunday School is so unreal!' or 'It's all so irrelevant!' It could be that the church is using inappropriate teaching methods in its children's groups, such as not relating what the children are doing in church to the activities and teaching methods they receive in school. Similarly, youngsters over the age of twelve need discussions and projects which enable them to use their own resources and learn from the experiences of others. Churches need to take stock of their activities and take responsibility when they fail young people. They must be aware constantly of the challenges and skills that are needed to keep their youngsters interested and stimulated.

So before leaping to the worst conclusion, Christian parents should listen to their teenagers' grouses and check with them that they have heard correctly. Get the facts, not just the feelings; then, if it is an important issue that has been raised, pass it on to the relevant person in church. Too many children leave the church because they are not listened to by the adults there. They feel that their views or problems are not worth anything and, consequently, that they themselves are not valued or respected.

Once your adolescent's mind is made up, however, and she decides not to come to church anymore, it is pointless to pursue the matter. Having established that nothing can be done to put things right, I suggest that it is best for parents to respect their child's wishes. To keep making her feel guilty or to sit in judgement on her will not prove helpful: your teenager must *want* to attend church. A more positive response on your part would be to invite her occasionally to a special service. You never know, she may surprise you one day and say, 'Yes!'

And finally...

As all these new influences now come into play, you will need to take a step back – not a step out of the picture, you're very much needed! – and adjust your position. This is easier said than done, but it may help if you accept that friends of your son or daughter will invariably have more influence than you. Don't rubbish them and don't do battle with your children over them. Try to avoid an inquisition every time an incident occurs. Let your child tell you in his own way and share with you what *he* wants to share. Finally, see your teenager as a part of your life not the whole of it and re-adjust your time and attention accordingly.

'Letting go' affects every aspect of the lives of both parents and adolescents. If we, as parents and carers, have done our job effectively, there should be no lasting major traumas: this process, with all its attendant difficulties will take its natural course, leaving the parent–child relationship intact. If there is a good foundation to fall back on there is no reason why it shouldn't be maintained. If, however, communication and understanding have always been difficult, family relationships will need to be worked at. But the rewards of doing this will far outweigh the stresses and strains experienced along the way.

3

Negotiating the bumps

Mutual trust and respect go a long way in pouring oil on the troubled waters of adolescence. As parents and carers, we know that we cannot demand the respect of our children, though we may desire or expect it: respect is a natural response to what they see in us. Cast your mind back to your own schooldays and think of the teacher you respected and trusted most. What qualities did she have? I guess words such as 'encouraging', 'fair', 'good at discipline' and 'authoritative' would come to mind. These qualities worked because the teacher was confident in her ability to use discipline and authority properly and not to abuse it. The same principle applies to parents.

Discipline and authority are not relinquished when your children become teenagers: they are still required to establish boundaries, to create a secure environment and to manage unacceptable behaviour within the family unit. Take care, though, to differentiate between discipline and dictatorship. The latter will only provoke a rebellious attitude or, worse still, induce cowed submission while feelings of rebellion are buried until such time as they erupt in later life, often with disastrous results.

Resorting to the well-worn 'Go to your room!' loses its momentum when the accused spends most of his time there anyway! How then can discipline be exercised without committing intellectual and emotional suicide? How can authority be maintained without a superior attitude of 'I'm right, so do as I say and don't question me!'? The phrase 'Do it because I say so!' is often the easiest for parents to use when they are frustrated at not being able to find the words to explain effectively *why* they are making a request. It is, however, a pretty weak basis for argument! Much better to take time to talk things through together and then make a firm request.

This chapter will attempt to outline choices in the ways we talk with and listen to our children. We need to establish a framework for effective communication that reduces (even if it does not eliminate!) the hassle and confusion. So often listening is sacrificed because we are too busy doing all the talking. But listening is active too. If we do not listen properly, we might as well give up on the rest of what we do as parents. Let's begin then with exploring authority and where it is held.

Authority

Something happens when a confrontation takes place. Panic may set in as parents over-react to the idea that their authority is going to be challenged. Or they dig in their heels and become inflexible at the thought that anyone would question their parental power anyway.

Both views seem to assume that parental authority is fragile and can be lost. So let's straighten out the confusion by stating something that may seem obvious but which passes many parents by. Parents *have* authority. We don't have to find it or acquire it – it is there, God-given, handed over to us at the same time as our baby. It is a fact not a choice and needs to be accepted as such. We should certainly use this authority wisely, appropriately and with loving confidence, or it will be abused and rendered ineffective. Wise use of parental authority protects our children from physical harm – such as when we refuse to allow them to go to a certain club or event which has a bad reputation, or draw boundaries at anti-social behaviour. However, for parental authority to be adhered to, it must be used consistently and with respect. An offhand or ambivalent manner is unlikely to be taken seriously.

If we are confident in our parental abilities, this will probably not be too difficult. However, if we are troubled by insecurity and feelings of inadequacy, we may become overly dictatorial to compensate for our perceived shortcomings, and end up tyrannising our teenagers. Until now it may have been easy to assert that, because we are older, bigger and more articulate, our children should accept our position. This stance gets a little harder to push, though, when we are trying to exert authority over a six-foot son who can match us in verbal dexterity! Remember – the scenario is not about physical superiority but about who's really in charge!

House rules

It is not unreasonable to expect that anyone living under your roof should conform to realistic standards of behaviour or household rules. This is so in any establishment: where two or more people are gathered together, a sense of organisation is necessary to avoid conflict!

When your children reach adolescence, previous guidelines, such as putting the toys away before bedtime (now more likely to be CDs, magazines and odd items of clothing left in a chaotic heap or distributed throughout every room in the house!) may become outdated. Don't shy away from establishing a new set of guidelines to accommodate the changing needs of the family. Every family unit is unique and will have different rules to enable it to run smoothly, and each parent will have their own level of tolerance. I could cope when our two teenagers brought home extra people for meals and to stay; but two stereos in different rooms blasting out different music took me beyond my limits!

If a few practical examples of how to establish guidelines would help, then the following random sample may start you thinking. They may seem very basic and obvious, but it is surprising how much they help to eliminate stress.

- When your son or daughter is going out in the evening, establish where they are going and when they expect to return. Ask them to give you a 'courtesy' phone call if they wish to extend their time out. Make sure they always have a phone card so that they can use the phone without any cash. Otherwise there will always be the excuse that they didn't have any change.

- Older teenagers may have their own set of house keys, but the trend now is to sleep over at friends' houses. Ask your son or daughter to phone before a certain time if they are not coming home, and to let you know where they can be contacted. *You* can then get to sleep without waiting anxiously for the sound of the key in the lock.

- It is infuriating to prepare a meal and then have your seventeen-year-old not turn up to eat it. Ask him to let you know well in advance if he wants meals or not: it will save you getting angry and give you the choice of whether or not to have food available.

- The meal has ended and the kitchen cleared. Then fifteen minutes later your offspring moves in. Crumbs appear on every visible surface. (How does one slice of toast still remain intact after making so many crumbs?) Sauce bottles sit on the counter with their tops off, and half-empty cans of beans lurk nearby. To cap it all, newly-dirtied plates are flung with merry abandonment into the sink. If your child is feeling kind and co-operative, he may half-immerse the dishes in cold water under the misguided assumption that this is helpful! If you own a dishwasher, adopt the rule that all dishes are to be put in that; if not, they must be washed up and put away, and the kitchen surfaces wiped over.

- If your youngsters bring friends home when you are not there, make sure they are aware of areas in the house that are *not* accessible to them. While hospitality should be encouraged, a certain amount of privacy is not too much to ask for. After all, you don't entertain your friends in your teenager's territory! Don't take this too far though – your home is also your teenager's and he should have the freedom to invite people back.

- Homework is often an issue fraught with problems. Encourage your child to do it at certain times, and provide an environment that is conducive to study. Don't expect all children to be the same, though, and allow for differences in temperament. Some find it easy to work to an orderly regime; others actually work better under pressure and can cope with leaving everything to the last minute. Let your child determine what works for him, and don't worry. Grades and teachers' comments will be a guide to how things are really going. Ultimately, it is your child's motivation that gets things done, not yours. A chat about how difficult it is to get down to study will probably bear more fruit than constant reminders shouted up the stairs.

Parents may moan about their home being treated like a hotel as their teenagers spend more and more time in the world outside. To do so is healthy and normal. However, even hotels have rules, and agreeing on some basic expectations is a way of ensuring harmony when your teenager *is* at home. If the house is a constant source of conflict, she certainly won't want to stay long anyway.

Testing the boundaries

Boundaries are established so that people know where the line is and can determine what is and is not acceptable. While it may seem rigid to adhere to them, boundaries provide a sense of security for all concerned. Goal posts that keep moving do not help to sustain trust or to encourage consistency in the relationship between you and your adolescent. It has already been acknowledged that the internal world of the emerging adult is changeable. One minute your teenager seems grown up, demanding independence and resenting any one who restricts this. The next, he is just an uncertain child needing support and guidance. In the muddle, firm guidelines are one of the consistent areas of his life. An absence of boundaries does not lead to freedom but to confusion and insecurity, which is extremely scary.

From time to time your child will test the boundaries you have set. Take your mind back – the process started with the little hand tentatively reaching out for something which you had said 'No' to. The little will of iron then thought, 'Perhaps Dad will change his mind. I'll have another go!' Full marks for persistence and effort, but if children perceive boundaries as sometimes being there and other times not – depending on the mood and tolerance level of their parents – they will continually try to beat down their parents' resistance and mould them to fit their own desires.

The same applies to adolescents – boundaries must be established and maintained. But if you are feeling depressed because your teenager constantly kicks against the boundaries you have set – relax. This process, however wearing for everybody involved, is actually a healthy activity! Boundaries are there to be pushed against so that they can be identified. Your child won't understand their significance unless they are aware of them. In their book, *Families and How to Survive Them*, Cleese and Skynner reinforce this concept:

You don't develop your muscles by relaxing or taking the line of least resistance. You struggle against some resistance – lift heavy weights, push against an obstacle.

Parents are needed as a force that their teenagers can push against in order to develop.

If they (parents) adjust to the young people's demands to try to please them … they'll not only end up feeling even more inadequate and in the wrong, they'll actually be providing the wrong response.

If children can't rebel safely at home where the limits are known, they will probably try to get the response they are seeking outside the home, perhaps with catastrophic results.

While consistent boundaries are not just desirable but necessary, we must be careful to hold this in balance. Too many rules and regulations – especially unnecessary ones with no room to negotiate – will have the effect of making your son or daughter feel that it is not worth trying to stick to them: the task is too formidable and they will always fail. Living life forever on a tightrope of anxiety in case rules are broken will only have the effect of producing a severely damaged adult who cannot break free from a regimented and highly structured lifestyle. Parents must be alert to spot when rules do not serve any really useful purpose or are just there to make them feel powerful. For rules to be effective, they need to be few, clear, and relevant!

So keep in mind the need to have a balanced perspective, and seek wisdom and guidance in achieving the right measure of authority and flexibility. While the Bible instruction (Ephesians 6:1–4) that children must obey their parents is often quoted, the counterpart to this teaching is easily overlooked: parents are instructed not to provoke their children to anger. Both sides share responsibility for the relationship between them.

Effective communication

What happens if your teenager refuses point-blank to adhere to family rules that are reasonable and fair? It may be that these rules have been part of your family life for a long time and, for your offspring, they no longer seem relevant.

Negotiation is key to keeping family rules up to date with the changing life of your children. As you handle this situation, bear in mind that no one wins in an atmosphere of antagonism or suspicion, so you will have to opt for diplomacy. Whatever you do, hold on to your self-esteem, because if that goes you will be at a disadvantage from the start! Ask your teenager what he would like changed in order for harmony to be restored. Then say what would make life easier for *you*, and why. The key here is that you are listening to your child and (hopefully) he is listening to you. Try not to shout and get angry as this will only worsen the situation – you will both wind up frustrated and nothing will be achieved. If you both try to listen and understand the other's point of view, maybe a mutually agreed arrangement can be reached. This solution may not be ideal, but it is workable, allows you to stay in control and lets neither side feel that they are being imposed upon by the other.

When your child was younger, boundaries were usually established entirely on parental terms; now that your child is an emerging adult, mutual agreement becomes more appropriate. For example, while you must respect the boundary of their territory (usually their bedroom), you have the right to expect the same of them when you are in your room having a moment's peace.

Our ability to interact with others determines whether we go through our lives communicating effectively or not. No end of misunderstandings occur simply because we do not check what we have heard. In every message there can be three components: what we think we have said, what we have actually said, and what was heard. No wonder we so often get it wrong! To understand others and to be understood ourselves, we need to ensure that we are consistent and honest in the way we give out information. We often make assumptions or endow our listener with (unrealistic) powers to pick up unsaid messages.

Listening is not a passive activity. (Unless you count the 'Yes' or 'No' or 'Fine by me' grunts that emerge from behind the newspaper!) Listening demands concentration and is often hard work. The rewards of being listened to and understood are enormous, and listening is a good way of effectively building up a relationship. Pause for a moment now and think about the day you have just had. How many times were you given someone's complete attention? When you were, didn't it make you feel valued?

When children reach adolescence, their patterns of communication change. The 'chatterbox' may suddenly turn into the strong, silent type, and monosyllabic exchanges take the place of conversation. The lively chats you once had on the journey back from school or over the kitchen table become rare, and it can often hurt to see friends being on the receiving end of all the enthusiasm instead of you! Or you may find that the opposite happens: you and your teenager start to discuss things in a way that is stimulating and rewarding. If so, great. Keep it up and value it – it is precious.

Someone who has done much work on parenting is Dr Thomas Gordon. I have used some of his material in parenting courses I have run and would readily endorse many of his theories. In his book, *Parent Effectiveness Training*, he suggests that there are three styles of ineffective parenting:

- the *dominant* parent who always has to win;

- the *permissive* parent who ensures that the child always wins;

- the *oscillating* parent who changes from one position to the other.

I would imagine that most parents fall into the last category, which is simply confusing to everyone. We seem to expect that in every argument there will be a winner or a loser; but this sets up a dynamic between parent and child which is confrontational. Dr Gordon quotes a mother who told him, 'I try to be permissive with my children until they get so bad I can't stand them. Then I feel I have to change and start using my authority until I get so strict I can't stand myself.' Sound familiar? How then can we construct an effective way of managing conflict *without* winners or losers?

Acceptance

How we respond to a particular situation is usually influenced by our feelings. If we are relaxed and life is relatively good, we are better able to cope with the situations and the people that we encounter in the world around us; our acceptance level rises. Conversely, if we are feeling stressed and negative about ourselves, our ability to cope can collapse quite dramatically! Our non-acceptance level will be more to the fore. We could all perhaps identify with the following scenario.

You have just got home from work. The traffic was terrible and there is loads to do before you go to that meeting at 8.00. While you're cooking supper the phone rings and, when you finally hang up, you feel squeezed and pressurised. It is at this moment that your teenager chooses to hover around, trying to ask you a question about homework.

'Not now! I'm busy and I haven't got time! Go and ask someone else. Or, better still, make yourself useful and do something to help!'

'You're *always* too busy! You're never interested in me. I don't know why I bother!' – SLAM!

Yes, it happens a lot – communication breakdown when Mum's or Dad's response has been totally misunderstood by the child on the receiving end. Our response is invariably influenced by the mood we are in. The real message – 'I *do* want to help you, but I'm stressed out. Can we arrange another time, maybe after we've eaten?' – gets lost. The result? Well, *they* stomp off feeling rejected and *you* end up feeling awful. Well, don't be overwhelmed with guilt! When we are not functioning on all batteries, things often slip out that we would otherwise have thought about more carefully.

It is helpful for parents to see their children as separate from themselves, having their own identity. We are with our children while they experience their problems, but we are not joined to them. We have to suspend our own thoughts and feelings so that we can hear properly what theirs are. Teenagers want most of all to be understood and to have their feelings acknowledged. Ultimately, with help, they want to sort out their *own* confusion; but this will not happen until their parents learn genuinely to value what they say.

To communicate effectively, parents must *want* to listen to their children. They will know instinctively if Mum or Dad is only pretending to give them attention. Furthermore, you must be able to accept your child's feelings honestly, whatever they may be and however much they differ from your own point of view. If, for example, your teenager complains he is being ignored by his classmates at school, it is probably unproductive to say, 'Don't be silly, of course they like you. It'll be all right tomorrow.' This doesn't address the real issue and, as well as labelling your child 'silly', you have discounted his feelings and put forward your own instead.

In my experience, children open up conversations and articulate anxieties in their own time and place. Parents need to be prepared for all eventualities – these talks can happen late at night, in the kitchen, at the top of the stairs or sitting on the end of your bed! (Many a time my husband and I have ended up practically 'falling off our perches', trying desperately to stifle the odd yawn!) It costs time and energy, but this is the sacrificial love demanded of parents. Being willing to listen and to accept builds bridges across many areas of friction and difficulty, and the fact that you were ready to take the time will never be forgotten.

Whose problem is it anyway?

Breaking down barriers to communication is made much easier by identifying who actually owns the problem! Is it my problem, is it my son's or daughter's problem, or is it a shared one? We need to learn how to tell the difference or we risk losing focus and achieving nothing.

> I own the problem when a situation or behaviour causes a problem to me but not to my child. The young person owns the problem when a situation or behaviour causes a problem to him but not to me, and it is only a shared problem when the situation or behaviour causes an individual problem to each of us. (From *Parent Effectiveness Training*, Dr Thomas Gordon.)

Identifying who owns the problem enables it to be dealt with quickly rather than to rumble on causing frustration and anger. Let's look at some examples.

A parent says to his son, 'You look dreadful with your hair like that. You really need to get it cut – it's all lank and greasy!' This is a problem for the parent. The teenager probably thinks his hair looks fine and wonders why Dad is making such a fuss! But Dad has difficulty accepting his son's long hair because it interferes with his own value system.

Your daughter is dreadfully upset because she has nothing to wear to the party and, of course, she can't wear the jeans you bought last month because they're not 'in' now. This is your daughter's problem – you, no matter how hard you try, can't understand what all the fuss is about!

'Why won't you let me go to the disco? All my friends are going.'

'Because I've heard what goes on at that place, and you're under-age anyway! It makes me worry about you.'

The problem is now a shared one. Both parties have strong feelings about it and both arguments feel logical to the person owning them. It is only when a new decision or outcome can be reached, using the skills of negotiation and diplomacy I outlined earlier, that a solution will become apparent.

A major obstacle to effective communication is blame. We all know how it feels to have someone accuse us: 'You shouldn't have done that!' 'What did you say *that* for?' 'Now look at what you've done!' We feel guilty and give up, or go on the defensive, with the result that the real point gets lost.

John is listening to his stereo at full volume in his room, which is directly above the sitting room. Dad yells up the stairs, 'John, are you deaf or something? Turn that noise off! You've got no consideration for others. We can't hear ourselves think down here!'

This approach is likely to invite a resentful, unco-operative response. If he owned that the problem belonged to him – using an 'I' message and being clear about why he wants quiet – Dad could go some way towards improving communication between John and himself.

'John, can you turn the music down? I am trying to talk to your mother and I can't hear. I'd like less noise!'

By openly acknowledging how we feel, by saying 'I' rather than 'You' when we discuss a point of disagreement with another, we don't leave the person feeling attacked or 'got at'.

I hope that the comments I have made in this chapter will help you to dismantle some of the blocks that get in the way of communicating with your adolescent. They may even help in other relationships too! Remember, behaviour patterns rarely change overnight. It takes time and practice; but what seems new will gradually become more familiar with time – and, above all, with listening!

4

Self-image and value

During the significant years of adolescence, a very confusing phenomenon takes place which often puts me in mind of those little houses containing two 'weather-people'. You remember them, I'm sure – they feature in the sort of seaside gift shop that the children drag you into when it is raining! One weather-person popped out when it was fine, the other emerged when it was cold and rainy. What never failed to amaze me as a child was that it was always one *or* the other, not both. This seemed to suggest that the weather was either going to be disastrous or delightful! Such was the analytical nature of my eight-year-old mind.

However, the more I picture our little weather-house, the more I am convinced that the people who popped in and out were adolescents! The sharp contrast of mood seems to mirror teenage years. One moment thundery blackness descends and communication shuts down; then the sun comes out – suddenly all is sweetness and light, with no visible reason as to why the change has taken place. One piece of advice here – never ask, 'Why can't you always be like this?' Because, in truth, adolescents are as confused as their parents. They don't know!

Many of the people I see in my work share this confusion. On the surface everything seems fine. They have loving families, successful businesses, and would appear to be easily able to work through the problem they have come to discuss with me. It is not long though before an underlying problem emerges – low self-esteem. This usually has its origins in an earlier part of the person's life, and is rooted inevitably in the way he was assured of his worth, or otherwise, within the family.

Self-esteem and confidence are two of the most problematic issues in adolescence. There may be a show of 'I'm coping' – and, indeed, many young people are confident and do cope. But many parents would benefit from exploring what they can do to contribute to (though not inflate) their children's confidence and to give them a firm, positive foundation for all that surrounds them in life today. In this chapter we will be highlighting skills that may be used to restore an ego which has been damaged through constant 'putting down' or neglect. No matter how you have failed as a parent, this is a chance to start again, to build up your teenager's self-image and to give a little attention to your own as well!

Affirmation

I remember an incident from my own childhood when I had come top of my class in English – quite an achievement for me! I beamed with pride as I handed my school report over to my father. I don't know what I expected, perhaps a hug or a 'Well done!' After what seemed a long silence, I tentatively said, 'I did really well in English, didn't I?' I got a stern rebuke for being so full of myself, and a lecture followed on how bad it was to give myself praise, as others should be left to do that. (The trouble was that those 'others' didn't either!) My father's closing remark – 'Perhaps you can feel pleased if you constantly keep to this standard' – left me feeling even more anxious and deflated. Compliments in my family were thin on the ground because they were seen as unnecessary and an encouragement to pride and vanity. Don't get me wrong – my father loved me dearly and thought he was doing me good by restraining his praise in this way. But it was many years before I could accept compliments and enjoy them.

The Victorian age contributed much that was good. But repressive attitudes – which were strictly adhered to, especially amongst the middle classes – did much to discourage any form of self-expression and prevented people from having a balanced, joyful, healthy attitude to self. We have, thankfully, moved on – not just in society, but in the Christian subculture too. However, some of these outdated modes of thinking still remain, with the result that many young adults are confused about how to be themselves and are in danger of becoming replicas of their parents, suffering the same doubts and kinds of repression. Giving children permission to be confident in their own personalities, those bestowed on them by God, is one of the most important things parents can do. Often such permission is withheld and the child's need to be recognised as a human being in his own right ignored.

We all need recognition. If we don't get it, we die physically or emotionally. If a baby is not given attention when she cries for feeding and comfort, she will not survive. If a child is not given recognition for who he is rather than what he does, he will not thrive. We all need unconditional acceptance. 'I love you.' 'You're great!' 'You mean so much to me.' I am constantly amazed at how many parents rarely give this affirmation to their children because they feel embarrassed or clumsy at voicing approval. If this is something that you as a parent identify with – and you don't affirm or encourage your teenager enough – then start now! You may feel self-conscious at first, but don't stop. It will get easier, especially when you see the results. Your son's or daughter's initial response may be unrewarding. After all, they haven't had encouragement for a long time! They may be embarrassed too. But, whatever the outward reaction, you can be sure that inwardly they feel good about being valued. Who doesn't?

If you are still not convinced that affirmation is a good thing, take your model from Psalm 145, where David praises God for who he is, not just for what he has done – a wonderful example of unconditional affirmation.

Richard was seventeen and studying for a couple of 'A' levels. He was not particularly academic but could expect to get reasonable enough passes to go to college. He appeared withdrawn when I spoke to him, and had only limited social contact and few friends. He had been told since childhood that if you want to succeed as a person you have to achieve. But the standards set by his parents had always been beyond his reach. Falling short of these, he felt he was a failure. There was never any recognition for who he was, only for his academic success, so the pressure to please his parents became a constant source of stress. He grew up believing that he was only acceptable to them when he fulfilled their desires. I last heard of him when he started college. Here was an individual with the potential to become a workaholic, driven by the desire to achieve. It was the only way of life he knew.

Unconditional recognition is the sort of affirmation that builds us up, and we need it all through our lives. Conditional recognition implies that we always have to *do* something in order to feel worthy. It is all too easy to slip into the habit of saying to your child, 'You're really nice when you're clean and neat' or 'I'm pleased with you when your room is all tidy.' (This is rare!) We all, of course, say things like this sometimes, but we need to balance them with statements which have no conditions attached.

I have given verbal responses as examples, but a hug, a kiss and a smile are all types of unconditional love and are just as effective. However, don't forget the down side. Frowns or 'put-downs' communicate negatives which can stay with a child and, if repeated often, make him feel totally useless and ready to give up.

Even though your adolescent's behaviour may be less

than desirable; even if they look extremely weird at times; even if their mood swings have you running to keep up: remember, your child is still a person worthy of your time and your respect, and deserving of understanding. You may not find their behaviour attractive, but never let them forget that you accept and love them. You may be left in the kitchen with steam coming out of your ears (metaphorically speaking!) after the last confrontation; but take a deep breath and recognise the little child inside the emerging adult. That child needs constant reassurance as well as discipline and boundaries.

That child is present in you too, and also needs reassurance that she or he is valued and respected. This is difficult when you are constantly being challenged or rubbished. A parent once stated in exasperation to her teenager, 'You may be confused but so am I! I haven't been the parent of a six-teen-year-old before – it's a first for me too!' Feelings of inadequacy are shared, so don't come on too heavy in order to cover yours up!

Exams!

In July and August each year, the media present us with tragic stories of teenage depression and suicide, often resulting from failure to obtain the expected grades in 'A' level examinations. Yes, 'A' levels are without doubt the most demanding exams routinely taken. Because of all the other stresses on the adolescent, exam time is a highly concentrated period when achievement may be the primary concern of both children and their parents.

I have often thought that character-building is just as important as academic achievement, if not more so. Of course, standards are important and we need aims to work towards; but standards can be given such prominence that they have the effect of intimidating young people, whose expectations of their achievements may be far more realistic than those of their parents. When talking to others about

51

your child's fantastic A grades (all seemingly achieved with minimum effort), and of his golden future, take care to notice who is likely to hear. Someone may be in the next room with knuckles clenched white, endeavouring to make sense of a text book that others have found a doddle! As he hears once again that he is expected to do brilliantly, your teenager may know that he hasn't a hope. Listening to parents saying such things over and over again can badly undermine self-confidence and make your son or daughter terrified of failure.

Children need to be valued for who they are, not how they measure up. Make sure that you affirm your teenager's individual gifts whether he is academic or not. In the end, a well-developed, mature character is of far more value to your offspring and to society than exam results. If this can be twinned with an active brain, fine – but an arrogant, egotistical genius does no one any favours!

Society today appears to esteem further education and academic qualifications out of all proportion to their real value. There are many gifted people around who left school at sixteen and who really enjoy life at work. If your child shows no desire to go to college or just isn't suited to an academic life, then take the time to discover with him the areas where he can shine in his own right and express his own personality. Some youngsters show great aptitude for using their practical or creative skills, or have a real talent in communicating with people and serving others. Parents may fall into the temptation of seeking to fulfil their own desires by projecting them onto their children and expecting them to succeed where they may have failed. It is therefore vital to listen to what your teenager is saying about himself and his future – it is all too easy to compete with other parents over your children's achievements. Churches too can get caught up in the competition to achieve academically, and then wonder why they attract only the middle classes and lose so many young people. There is no room for pride or class

distinctions in God's kingdom, and Christians should celebrate diversity.

Disruptions to the parenting pattern

It would be useful at this stage to look at two areas which
may surface in the adolescent years and affect youngsters'
self-esteem and search for identity – step-parenting and
adoption. The effect on the family of divorce and bereavement will be dealt with more extensively in another chapter.

Let's take adoption first. I know many families who have
adopted, where the child has been aware since he could
understand of the special circumstances surrounding his
arrival into the family. The whole family unit is happily
bonded. I'm sure you can identify families like this – run-of-
the-mill and ordinary, with no obvious problems. However,
in others, adolescence – with its search for identity – may
spark a desire to find out more about a natural mother and
father. The teenager may want to establish a sense of belong-
ing, a rootedness which in no way interferes with her being
part of the adopted family. Rather the adopted child is simply trying to discover her place in the larger scheme of things
and to identify her origins.

Legally, it is the child's right to initiate contact with the
natural parent, but this can sometimes prove traumatic.
Hurdles may be put in the way: the natural parent may not
wish to establish contact; or, if contact is made, the reality
may be considerably different to what either the child or the
parent expected. This can bring issues of loss more keenly to
the surface. Expectations and fantasies may have been built
up through the years. Idealised images may have replaced
flesh-and-blood reality, especially if the relationship between
the child and the adoptive parents is less than satisfactory.
When a natural parent refuses to see their son or daughter, it
may compound already established feelings of rejection
within the child, though often the reason for not wanting to
establish contact is not a desire to reject but a fear of causing

disruption to a new family with children who may not know of a previous brother or sister. The natural parent may also be reminded of a painful time in their life, a time of guilt, loss and overwhelming confusion and pain. To open these wounds again may be more than they feel they can cope with. I have known, however, of reunions where all goes well and the adopted child forms a new extension to the established family unit, with enjoyable visits and a growing relationship with all the new family members.

If you are the parents of an adopted child, you may be aware of many emotions yourself, particularly fear of the unknown and anxiety that your child will find their natural parents and love them more than they love you (irrational, but easy to understand). Whatever your feelings, it is vitally important to stand alongside your son or daughter while they consider the implications of initiating contact. They are not rejecting you – you are the parents who have brought them up, loved them and cared for them. They are only taking a step in their development towards adulthood.

Sadly, at these times a certain amount of hostility may be directed towards the adoptive parent. If home life is a battleground and communication has broken down, your son or daughter will need to put the blame somewhere, to find a reason why life hasn't turned out the way they wanted it to. Parents can be wonderfully convenient scapegoats. Accusations like 'I wish you weren't my parents – my real mother/father would never have treated me like that!' may be used as weapons in any confrontations that arise between you. Making someone a scapegoat is a way of putting negative feelings in a place where they can't be challenged, and leaves a trail of emotional chaos in its wake.

Whatever the adopted child decides to do and whatever the outcome, any disruption to the adoptive family usually settles down eventually. As the adolescent approaches adulthood, his sense of identity becomes more established and he has a greater feeling of security with, hopefully, a sense of direction and purpose. A couple we have known since child-hood adopted several children, and could probably write a book on their traumas and colourful experiences. There was a time, not so long ago, when family life was taken to its lim-its, and the emotional pain caused by their adolescents was almost too much to bear. However, they hung on and came out the other end older but much wiser. Only recently they were able to testify what a good relationship they now had with their adult sons and daughters.

Similar patterns of scapegoating may occur when remar-riage brings another adult into the family unit. When a par-ent has died or divorce has taken place, there is often a period when members of the family draw comfort and secu-rity from each other. Then, suddenly, another person arrives on the scene. This intruder may have been around in the background for some time, and everything was OK. But, as soon as he or she becomes a member of the family, the dynamics change. The family may have adjusted to their loss and settled down into a familiar pattern. Accommodating a new person with a new role can prove very difficult to a child of any age. It is especially difficult for the adolescent.

Once all its members are bonded, the new family can be a source of encouragement and support. However, there may be a few hurdles to negotiate first. Along with the usual teenage difficulties comes the problem of the step-parent's authority, which can cause resentment and hostility in the young person. Cries of 'You can't tell me what to do – you're not my dad!' and 'My mum would have let me do that – she trusted me!' are common, and will try the most patient step-parent who is doing all they can to get the relationship right. Someone has to carry the anger and hurt that the child feels as a result of the break-up of the marriage or the death of a parent. It is too risky to blame the parent who remains, so the 'wicked step-mother/father' is a convenient person on whom to dump all the rubbish!

When this happens, it can threaten the most confident

and loving person, who probably never imagined that it would be so difficult. The adolescent is confused too because, in his heart, he probably wants to establish a good relationship with the new parent; yet, irrationally, he may feel that he can't love you without slighting the parent who has gone. Children are inclined to be very loyal, and seeing their mother or father enjoying life again and, horror upon horrors, actually sharing a bedroom with this new family member, can seem like betrayal.

If you are in this situation and are struggling with establishing your place in the new family, take heart – a day will come when you start to see an improvement. In the meantime, the following hints may help:

- Don't try too hard! Whilst you want to be accepted and liked, don't push too much. Your behaviour may seem patronising and forced.

- Show a real (not artificial) interest in your step-children and what *they* are interested in.

- Don't undermine or criticise your spouse in front of your step-children. They will resent you doing this.

- In everything you do, try to communicate the love, care and respect you have for your new husband or wife, and for your step-children too.

- When problems occur, make sure that you and their mother or father talk things through first, if you take different positions on an issue. It is better to resolve your differences in private than in front of your children. This, of course, applies to *all* families.

- Include your step-children in family decisions. This will help them feel that their needs are important and listened to.

- Just in case you missed it earlier – don't try too hard!

Self-esteem and identity are vitally important in this transitional stage of development. There is no foolproof method of circumventing all the traumas and doubts that your teenager will encounter, but without working through the difficulties, there will be no arrival at a whole and rewarding adulthood. It was the poet Blake who stated that 'Without contraries is no progression' and we certainly see many of these in the adolescent period!

Building a healthy self-image is not something that can be done in isolation. It requires affirmation and recognition from others. If we allow ourselves to be warmer and more giving in our appreciation and praise – not just in families but in schools, churches and industry too – we could make such a positive mark on our society. What a challenge!

One of the family

To me you are special.
Special, because you belong to me, and are mine.
The fact that I didn't give birth to you
    doesn't make me less of a mother,
    or you my daughter.
For mothering is far more than birth,
    and growing is something
    that we can experience together,
    at our own pace.
I longed for you,
    though I didn't know then your face.
And when at last you were chosen
My life took on a new dimension.
We were a family.
Now as you continue to develop,
I see mirrored in your personality
    a reflection of our own ways.
And a bond has been created –
    of love, warmth and security.

    (From *The Gift of a Child*, Claire Short (ed),
    Lion.)

5

Sexuality

There comes a moment in every parent's life – that moment of revelation when realisation dawns that your child is a child no more. The awkward bumps of puberty and early adolescence have turned into a mature adult body. And, no matter how gradually you have got used to the changes, it is still a jolt to see that your offspring is a young man or woman – and knows it! Sexuality has come of age!

This is perhaps one of the most significant events not only in the adolescent's life but in that of their parents too. By observing the emergence of their son or daughter's sexual identity, parents are inevitably confronted with their attitude towards their own! In this chapter we explore the different areas that come into prominence (if you will forgive the expression!) at this time. You may find they help you to reflect on your own sexuality too.

A positive sexual identity in its appropriate place is healthy and wholesome. It grounds other aspects of our personality and enables us to be confident and secure in the man or woman that we are. Conversely, a damaged or uncertain belief in our sexuality can invade and threaten many other aspects of our personality.

As children grow up, they look to their role models – their parents – for affirmation and teaching about being the person, and the sex, they are. This may seem obvious, but there are countless people in the world today who have never been given 'permission' to be male or female, who remember occasions when they overheard a parent telling someone that they really wanted a child of the opposite sex. Throwaway comments like these can do a great deal of damage, suggesting that somehow the child has got it wrong and been a disappointment from day one! Parents are getting better at dealing with the biological facts of life, but often miss out on the emotional side of affirming sexuality.

Sexuality is often confused with sex. However, whereas sex involves a physical expression of our sexuality, sexuality can be expressed in other ways. We express positive sexuality when we acknowledge our gender and are at ease with it among both men and women, when we celebrate the feminine and masculine characteristics which make us different, as well as those we share. A negative attitude to our sexuality can bring about feelings of low self-worth, an inability to be at ease in the company of the opposite sex, and difficulty in integrating our sexual identity with the rest of our personality.

Acknowledging sexuality

I have listened to many confused dads who one minute are perfectly relaxed about giving their daughters a cuddle, but, who, as their daughters grow into women, develop a phobic fear of showing *any* physical affection at all. Suddenly the goal posts have been moved; Dad is uncertain about his feelings; and the daughter who used to clamber on his lap for a cuddle seems alien. Nothing abnormal has happened, but coping with this transition is something that many mothers and fathers find mystifying. It is unfortunate if they manage to communicate their anxiety to an already confused adolescent! When a voluptuous daughter rushes downstairs in the new bikini she has just bought for the family holiday and enthusiastically asks, 'Mum, Dad, what do you think of this?', she can be forgiven for being perplexed when Dad changes colour and mumbles strangely, with panic written all over his face. Let's look then at what is going on.

Consciously, your daughter is asking for approval in a straightforward way. Unconsciously, she wants the most important man in her life to say that she looks lovely and to affirm her womanhood. Dad panics because he can't cope with the mixed-up feelings going on inside him. He doesn't really want to believe that his little girl has grown up into an attractive woman, and his defence is to deny that he has noticed. A dismissive 'Go and get some proper clothes on!' seems to come to him more easily than 'You look lovely!' His daughter ends up feeling embarrassed, rejected and frustrated at not getting recognition from the safe place she had expected. If this is reinforced repeatedly during her developing years, she will go elsewhere for affirmation.

It is important that mothers also tell their children that they look good and that they are proud of them. Feelings of envy – when a lithe, young body makes you conscious of the ageing process – are misplaced. It is vitally important that this time of awakening is recognised and sensitively managed by both parents. Don't forget, though, to hold to definite boundaries, to give your child lots of hugs and affection but in appropriate ways and at appropriate times.

Be positive with your children, help them to accept their bodies and their bodies' natural functions. Encourage a low key, matter-of-fact response to menstruation and 'wet' dreams, for they are the part of the body's ongoing development. Parents may need to liberate themselves from some of their own hang-ups about these things. Not so long ago, menstruation was called the 'curse' and was assumed to be a hush-hush topic, unsuitable for discussion when father was in the room. Nowadays, most boys are well-informed and quite relaxed about the subject, and television regularly shows advertisements for products related to menstruation. Don't then create a taboo of your own around this natural process, where your daughter can only tell Mum about the onset of her period and assumes that her dad and her brother are ignorant of such things, or that the subject is just not relevant to them. In some parts of France a bottle of champagne is opened when the daughter of the family has her first period to celebrate the fact that she has become a woman. You may feel this is a little over the top or a waste of good champagne, but perhaps we could all learn a little from such a positive parental attitude to God-given sexuality!

Sex education

From the onset of puberty, if not before, try to ensure that you as a parent (whether Mum or Dad) are at ease with and well-informed about sex education. It's good to have the attitude that questions on sexuality are a normal part of family life rather than something to dread. If this area is neglected or mismanaged during adolescence, and sex is never mentioned at home, the results can be damaging later on in life.

I saw Mattie over a period of two years. She had been married for some time and had two children. She had, however, never enjoyed sex, seeing it as a duty rather than a mutual pleasure, and was not orgasmic. In fact, despite her husband's constant reassurance and loving concern, she felt that her body was dreadful and that sex was dirty, disgusting and a chore – like cleaning the oven, only more frequent!

As therapy progressed, it became apparent that Mattie's negativity about herself and sex was inherited from her mother whom she had often heard discussing the trials of the physical side of her marriage on the phone to her sister, Mattie's aunt. At the onset of menstruation, her mother gave Mattie a packet of sanitary towels and said that she would now have the 'curse' every month and not to let anyone know. Mattie's mother was encouraging her daughter to develop a negative and pessimistic attitude to her body that would become firmly established before Mattie married.

It took time, patience and lots of permission for Mattie to feel good about herself and accept her sexuality as a positive aspect of her whole being. Not only did the relationship with her husband improve, but her whole personality changed. Like a butterfly emerging from its chrysalis, a more beautiful and confident Mattie emerged, determined not to make the same mistakes with her own daughter.

Sex education therefore begins at home, where information should be accurate and reliable. Sex should be put in the context of the whole person, with its positive aspects stressed and guidelines given to ensure that this wonderful gift is used well and your children protected as far as possible against its abuse and devaluation.

Media influence

If I were asked to single out one aspect of society today that pressurises and seduces young people, I would say, without any hesitation, that it has to be the media – television, magazines, newspapers and the cinema. As represented in the media, sex has become a commodity and, like most commodities, it is being marketed and targeted at the group from which it can make the most money – adolescents. The great deceit, however, is that sex is being sold in a harmful and destructive way to those whose powers of discernment are not yet fully developed.

Sex is a wonderful act, one of God's gifts to us to enjoy, but in the world of the media it is depicted as a disposable asset – easy come, easy go. It doesn't matter if you are not even in a relationship – the important thing is just to have sex with whoever you like, whenever you like.

My work dictates that I am virtually unshockable. It takes a lot to ruffle my feathers! I was, however, intensely angry when I recently did some research on magazines –

available at any newsagent – which were targeted at teenage girls aged thirteen and upwards. Specific advice on 'How to turn your boyfriend on' and 'How to dress to "pull" the blokes' seemed blatantly to ignore the fact that humanity is more than the sexual act and, that it is not the only way to relate to boyfriends or girlfriends. This anomaly has now been brought to the attention of the public by a member of parliament, but as yet no action has been taken to protect impressionable young people.

Magazines today sell on their 'sex' content. You only have to look at the covers: there aren't many that don't have at least one article on how to have better sex or become multi-orgasmic! Top fashion designers are now using thirteen- and fourteen-year-old girls to model overtly sexy clothes, their body language suggesting images of sexual activity. Pubescent girls appear on the covers of magazines that purport to be aimed at the 18+ age group, thus giving a very distorted message to the girls who actually buy them.

Eating disorders, such as bulimia or anorexia nervosa, are often the result of an obsessive need to distort the natural body image. Young girls may semi-starve themselves to achieve the thin, angular limbs of waif-like 'supermodels'. Boys too are becoming increasingly conscious of their image and want to have bodies like Keanu Reeves or members of the group Take That! The teenage sub-culture will dictate the 'in' shape and appearance, suggesting that anyone who doesn't conform is unacceptable and unattractive. Reassuring your daughter that she looks gorgeous as she is can fall upon deaf ears. Such is the power and strength of the media demon, seeking to distort and discourage individuality and self-acceptance.

If this happens to your child (it is usually daughters who are affected), don't hesitate to ask for help, not just for your teenager but for you too. The outward signs of eating disorders may be all too familiar, but the problem is not really physical though it manifests itself in this way. There may be deep-rooted emotional problems, perhaps focused on relationship difficulties within the family, that need to be uncovered.

The stress that eating disorders cause will certainly affect the whole family, and support may be obtained from Christian counselling agencies such as the Association of Christian Counsellors or, in the secular sector, the British Association for Counselling, and Relate. Your GP will also be able to let you know where to go to for specific advice relating to anorexia or bulimia.

The distortion of sex corrodes traditional values and promotes sexuality as cheap and worthless rather than as a God-given, healthy part of human nature, to be respected and valued. The effect that this fragmentation of the whole person has on any teenager can be devastating because, as we have seen earlier, image and identity are forming in this period. Impressionable youngsters can be forgiven for being confused and misled when there is so much pressure to confirm to the norms of society.

We cannot wrap our children up in cotton wool or shut their eyes to what they see everyday. But we can help them work out for themselves that they don't have to look or behave in the ways the media demands in order to be acceptable.

Pornography

Whilst teenage girls generally read magazines that focus on image and self-improvement, boys seem to bury their heads in more practical reading matter on music, bikes, computers or sport. These are usually littered around the house or sit happily on the bedside table with several brown coffee-mug ring-marks encircling every cover. No problem – you put them into a nice neat pile to make you feel better. (But before you know it, they have scuttled to every room in the house again, messy but inoffensive!)

For some mothers, however, an over-zealous tidy up will unearth magazines hidden away under the mattress or at the back of the wardrobe, where it is hoped that no duster or maternal hand will ever venture! Parents' reactions vary when soft porn or 'girlie' magazines are found, from anger, shock and horror to resigned acceptance. Do you shove them back and say nothing, or confront a mortified son when he arrives home and finds them on the kitchen table? Perhaps neither of these actions is helpful.

The vast majority of adolescent boys are curious about the female form and, especially before they become sexually active, have voyeuristic tendencies. This is perfectly natural, as is the surge of hormones that can accompany the thought and sight of attractive females! It is a well-known fact that men tend to be aroused by visual stimuli, whereas women respond more to touch and emotion. But while sexual attraction in itself is natural, the way that it is gratified may lead to a distorted set of values affecting a man's general attitude towards women.

You will probably get all kinds of excuses from your son when the magazines are discovered: 'They're not really mine – I'm just looking after them for a friend!' Or their friend has 'accidentally' left them and will collect them tomorrow. If your son does own up to buying them, appreciate his courage in admitting this and don't sabotage any hopes of further communication by blasting him out at this stage! The last thing he needs is for you to open the magazines in front of him and embark on a lecture complete with visual aids! You may both end up feeling humiliated and embarrassed. Perhaps a more useful approach is to enlist some help if you are a single parent, or make this a joint parental issue and tackle it together with your partner. It's not just your views that need to be heard, but your son's too. If you listen to what he has to say, he may be more prepared to listen to what you advise.

If you have brought your son up with respect for and appreciation of the human form and have stressed the importance of valuing a woman as a whole person, not just as a body, it could be that you only need to reinforce this message. You could discuss the contradiction between these values and the values of the magazines. In some cases, though, there may be a growing addiction on his part to this kind of 'soft' pornography, where the reader gets 'hooked' onto idealistic, distorted and aggressive images of women. These foster contempt and lead to a devaluation of women in general. The 'dark' side of the publishing industry exploits and deepens this dependency to sell more magazines. The long-term effects are disastrous. If a man is married, the sexual act may no longer be regarded as a mutual act of love and pleasure but simply as a way of receiving instant gratification, which eventually degrades both his wife and himself.

If you can relate to some of the above and your son is acknowledging that he has a problem with pornography, then you will need to be sensitive. Porn is a lonely, solitary activity, and making him feel humiliated and guilty will drive him further into his shell. Far better to build the positives, and talk through his feelings and thoughts about his problem. Put forward your views about the value that women deserve, about wholeness, respect and love. Allow him to see for himself how he is potentially sabotaging a fulfilling and satisfying sex life with a partner in the future. Check that your own relationship with your son is satisfactory and see how he is relating to his friends. And, if you are a dad, check that your relationship with your wife is one that demonstrates respect and love.

Pornography is rarely an isolated activity in its own right. It is much more likely to be a symptom of underlying anxiety or other problems, and is more prevalent among those who are lonely or who feel inadequate in the eyes of their peer group. By addressing the problem at its roots, the symptoms may disappear and other healthier activities take the place of unhealthy ones.

Masturbation

Masturbation is one of those 'hot potatoes' that is usually taboo in the Christian church. There is no explicit Bible teaching on the subject, and opinions vary even among Christians. As is often the case when this happens, people draw their own conclusions according to their own views and conditioning. In fact, almost all adolescents masturbate as a normal part of growing up. It is a harmless activity and usually provides an outlet for all the sexual feelings that are surging around, accompanied by extremely active hormone levels!

Masturbation does cause some problems, however. It may become obsessive and compulsive – not particularly likely in a healthy, outgoing teenager, but possible in a more withdrawn and solitary character who is unsure of his sexuality. (Masturbation is allegedly more common among boys.) The frequent accompaniment of pornography and erotic fantasy may bring about a heavy dependency on visual images for ejaculation, and often this intrudes into relationships later on.

If your teenager is using masturbation excessively (and accept the fact that often you won't know), then try to find out what is the underlying problem. Is it lack of friends, low self-esteem, boredom or difficulties your child is having at school or college? By focusing on an area that he has a degree of control over, your child is trying to address his needs; but he is doing so in a way that will leave him feeling more negative and unrewarded.

Masturbation often leads to a misplaced sense of guilt. Quite a large percentage of the people that I see with problems relating to their sexuality trace one of the root causes back to their guilt at being discovered masturbating when they were younger. The attitude of parents is vital and can influence their children well into adulthood. By accepting self-stimulation as a natural part of physical development, you will avoid making an issue of it, and as they grow into adults your teenagers may not feel the need for it. If, however, you become punitive and disapproving, you will inevitably prolong and intensify the underlying feelings which accompany masturbation, and guilt and shame will be taken on board inappropriately. Unconsciously, this will affect how the adult perceives sex and his or her own genitalia, and may bring about sexual dysfunction for fear of letting go and losing control.

Sexual orientation

In puberty and early adolescence, an attachment to another person of the same sex is, like masturbation, quite natural. After all, you know how this person acts, feels and thinks – it is easy to identify with him or with her. But sometimes over-identification takes place: the comfortable friendship changes and intense love takes its place. Powerful sexual feelings are aroused, and the young person may have fantasies about the other. If there is nowhere to go to be reassured that this is all part of the process of sexual development, the adolescent may be left in a highly anxious state and very confused about his or her sexual orientation.

It is helpful to distinguish here between the homosexual who has always been attracted to his or her own sex and the teenager who experiences these feelings in the process of developing a sexual identity which, by adulthood, is firmly established as heterosexual. Love is felt very keenly in adolescence, and society pressurises us continually to equate love with sex. Love, that warm, bonding appreciation of another, is not often valued in its own right. Boys can have a love for other boys, girls can love other girls, just as adults can love one another. Love is sharing ourselves with others. People can share a love which is deep and profound but not necessarily romantic. Many churches now see the value of showing appreciation by giving someone a hug and of being freer in affirming one another.

Society tends to devalue the purity of such *agape* love

and promote negative expressions of sexuality as fashionable. The more sexually outrageous and provocative someone is, the more attention and comment that person attracts from the media. Lesbianism has commanded much attention, on women's magazine covers, and in 'soaps' and television drama. Young people are increasingly exposed to the idea that being gay or bisexual is an option they can take if they choose, and are experimenting with their sexual orientation far more than even a few years ago.

There will always be those who develop a preference for people of the same sex and who struggle with this throughout their lives. If you have not had to experience this yourself, you may struggle to understand your child. It is often the case that parents are the last to know. The debate about whether homosexuality is genetic or conditioned, nature versus nurture, may never be conclusively proved. Many parents refuse to listen when their son or daughter discloses their homosexual orientation, probably because they do not want to believe it or face up to the implications.

If your child has had the courage to share with you, 'Mum (or Dad), I think I'm gay!', try not to dismiss their concern with comments like 'Of course you're not!' or 'How could you do this to us!' Instead, endeavour to listen with understanding, and explore with your child the reasons why he or she has come to that conclusion. I have known several situations where parents take on misplaced guilt, blaming themselves for 'getting it wrong'. These parents often need more help coming to terms with the situation than their adolescent.

If your child actively pursues a homosexual lifestyle and is over 18, there is little you can do about it – it is a choice that has been made by an independent adult. Try hard to keep the communication channels open. But if you find that the situation is causing you stress and anxiety, do seek support for yourself. Parents need to explore their own feelings in coming to terms with a child's homosexuality and should try to do so with an experienced counsellor or a trusted friend. A sensitive and wise approach on the part of the listener may be of great help.

In any large grouping of young people, there will inevitably be a section who believe they have a homosexual orientation. Care and understanding should be the primary concern of parents. After all, it is not the *orientation* but the *practice* of homosexuality that the Bible condemns. We must be a support to our children, not a stumbling block. If we respond with loving concern, they have every chance of emerging with wholesome and confident sexual identities.

6

Relationships

During the years of adolescence it is likely that your home will resemble a busy station, with people coming and going all the time. No sooner do you familiarise yourself with one set of names than you are presented with another. Some people just pass through; others become part of the furniture. Indeed, you may perceive in time that one particular friend is coming round more frequently, and their name seems to pop up in every conversation. Add to this long phone calls that have no direct purpose, and you will arrive at the very obvious conclusion: yes, your teenager has fallen in love – for the moment!

While this can be a cause for amusement at one level, the longer the relationship continues the greater the scope for anxiety in the parent. For while the teenager is sorting out his or her sexuality, Mum and Dad may be anxious about these two young people becoming involved together, both with soaring hormone levels and unreliable emotions! This is the stage when panic can set in as you go over in your mind all the things you have told them, and worry about all the things you may have left out!

It's back to trust and responsibility again. Parents can't

control their offspring's every action – they have to hand that responsibility over to them and hope they have taken in the values and standards passed on to them over the years. All the same, parents will probably worry about whether or not their teenagers are going further physically than their parental value system and Christian teaching say they should. The truth is that it is rare for youngsters to tell their parents the secrets of their love life, and you probably just won't know! It is certainly inappropriate to give them the 'third degree' every time they come home.

Instant gratification

The world today tells us that if we want something, we don't have to wait – we can have it *now*! If we don't have any money, well, we can get a loan. Everything is available – at a price. The concept of instant gratification encompasses all aspects of life, including sex. The message seems to be 'If it feels good, do it – as long you wear a condom.' Schools and colleges frequently put contraceptive slot-machines in both male and female cloakrooms. Society seems to be giving permission for young people to go ahead. Indeed, it is extremely rare these days to find youngsters in an established relationship that doesn't involve sex. This can put subtle pressure on Christian teenagers to go further than they feel is comfortable, so as to conform to what is expected and 'keep up' with their peers.

While society gives one set of rules, God gives another and, for the Christian, sex outside the trust and security of marriage is not an option (see 1 Corinthians 6:12-18 and Ephesians 5:3). However, this doesn't mean that Christians have it easy; far from it – they have the same passions and desires as anyone else. Most people feel that the Christian view is archaic and can't see the value of holding to it. But God's order is established to bring harmony and fulfilment, not misery and frustration. Let's now look at the positive aspects of waiting.

Many of the clients who come to me for counselling share the same sexual problem. The wife would really like more cuddling and non-sexual touch as part of the relationship alongside sexual activity; but the husband tends to see any form of prolonged physical contact as the green light for sex. What happens? Non-sexual affection and touch invariably stop so that no misunderstandings arise, and sex becomes an isolated activity with no time taken to enjoy leisurely caressing and cuddling at all. The majority of these couples have had a sexual relationship before marriage, have got used to having sex on demand, and have missed out on a vital part of communication and pleasure.

One positive aspect of having time together without sex is the opportunity to build up trust and security through non-sexual touch, to get to know each other within some limits and boundaries. This frees the relationship and allows each person to see the other as more than just a sexual partner. Many people, it seems, get married or start living together because the sex is fantastic. When reality starts to intrude or the sex isn't so good any more, they discover they have little in common with their partner – even their value systems may not be compatible.

Sexual security

There is a very real way in which we need to protect ourselves emotionally when it comes to sex. If every relationship someone has includes sex, he will carry around a lot of memories. When this person eventually does meet the one he wants to settle down with, emotions or problems involving previous partners may rob the new relationship of the distinctive quality of being special; for there *is* something very special about your first sexual partner satisfying you for the rest of your life.

Protection of our bodies is important too at a time when sexually transmitted diseases are on the increase. Parents must ensure that their teenagers are well-informed about AIDS, herpes and other sexual problems. A wealth of informative, easy-to-read books and leaflets are accessible in libraries or available from chemists and bookshops. Schools and educational health programmes are now bringing in experts or using videos to educate youngsters in these vital areas. But it is frightening how information tends to be ignored or forgotten when personal application is required. Your teenager sees the 'now' moment as the only one that matters. Furthermore, much teaching on sexual health is based on a secular philosophy, with little sympathy given to the Christian viewpoint. As a result, the latter needs to be reinforced elsewhere, at home and in church.

Privacy

Another area of difficulty is a practical one. Houses today seem to be built to a smaller scale with fewer rooms, so where does your child go with her boyfriend to be alone? Do you think she has the right to privacy, and how do you support this when the only available place is in her bedroom? It is often assumed that if they go to a bedroom, teenagers will be using every available moment to have sex. Many an anxious parent is fretting away downstairs imagining the worst, while upstairs the couple are listening to music, reading magazines or doing some other harmless activity, and sex is the last thing on their minds!

Parents must work out how they can negotiate this issue of privacy realistically with their offspring and still ensure that both sides are able to present their views. It helps if your son or daughter knows that you are on their side and not intent on taking away every bit of privacy they have.

Christian parents may find that it is in Christian homes that teenagers most often question the reasons for not having sex before marriage. In the light of present cultural attitudes, it will make sense to them that they express their love once they are committed to each other, and they may see no reason to wait. The views of Christian parents may come across as outdated and irrelevant in this day and age. Two strongly opposed value systems clashing with each other is not very conducive to compromise, and any discussion may leave your teenager even more entrenched in her own viewpoint.

There will always be opportunity for young people to have sex if they want to, and there is nothing parents can really do to prevent it happening (unless they lock their children up!). This may be hard for parents to take on board, and leave them feeling powerless and anxious about their offspring. But shouting and moralising will only fragment the relationship you already have with your child and cause an ever-widening gap between you.

Sexual activity

If your son or daughter has become sexually active at a relatively early age, despite your guidance, you may find yourself with hard decisions to make. Some parents just get angry and tell their children that they must stop having sex, as if that is the end of the matter. However, exploding with disapproval is likely to be of little value, as is burying your head in the sand. Forbidding your teenager to use contraception is even less helpful, as you will probably end up with an unplanned pregnancy on your hands. Far better to acknowledge what has happened and to ensure that contraceptive advice has been taken. This is difficult, but eminently more sensible than the alternative.

If your offspring is over eighteen, you may have to be prepared to accept that they have developed a different value system from yours. By all means let them know how you feel, but then leave the responsibility with them. You are not condoning or approving their activity but simply accepting that you now have limited control over their adult decisions. You do have the right, however, to expect that they do not sleep together under your roof. This would impinge upon *your* value system which they, in turn, should respect.

Deeper problems

Many of the situations we have covered so far could be seen as everyday ones which most families will encounter at one time or another. There are some, however, that produce deeper and more lasting effects, not just on the adolescent, but on the family too. The words that every parent probably dreads most are 'Mum, I'm pregnant' or 'Dad, I've got my girlfriend pregnant'. In the time it takes to utter such a memorable statement, the future seems to take a tumble and leave hopes and dreams in fragments.

Sadly, abortion figures for the UK are all too high. In 1994 statistics show that 3,246 abortions were performed on girls under the age of sixteen, and the figures leap to 25,223 on girls between the ages of sixteen and nineteen. Too often pregnancy counselling agencies seem to go straight to talking about abortion and miss out the choices available to the girl. Many women I have counselled cannot, despite the years and subsequent children, come to terms with the loss of their first child and regret that they ever had a termination. If we are to encourage young mothers to see their pregnancies through, we need to be ready – not just as individuals but as churches too – to ensure the well-being of the mother and baby, in practical and emotional ways.

A young adolescent pregnancy is a situation for which parents must share responsibility with their offspring. Your son or daughter will need your complete support to go through what could amount to many years of struggle. There is no doubt that keeping the baby will affect its grandparents' lives drastically too, especially if it is a daughter's who is still living at home. Just as you thought that days of baby-care were far behind, they become a noisy and demanding part of family life again. You will have your own feelings about this, and these will need to be worked through.

For Christian parents, the situation will raise such questions as 'How will the church react?' 'What will our friends think?' 'Will people see this as a reflection of the way we have brought our children up?' Even if these are not voiced, you may be sure that they are thought, and parents may be so preoccupied with outside perceptions and criticisms that they fail to address the needs and worries of their adolescent.

There may be several agendas running at this time: that of the parents of the pregnant girl, the young mother's herself, and – if he is willing to be involved – the boyfriend's and possibly his parents' too. These separate agendas will need to be openly discussed. Initial reactions on the part of both sets of parents may be anger, blame, guilt and despair, and these need to be dealt with so that the various parties can share practical love and mutual support.

Karen was fifteen, living at home with her mother – her parents having divorced when she was seven – and her sister and brother. Karen's mother needed to work full time and had a busy social life in the evenings, often leaving Karen to look after the younger ones. Karen was always blamed if anything went wrong, and had obviously been given too much responsibility too soon. When she started going out with Steve, who was her age, it was fun, and she loved all the attention he gave her. Within six months she was pregnant, and her mother was pressurising Karen to have an abortion. Karen was adamant that she wanted to keep the baby. It was hers – it would need and love her unconditionally, and would give her significance. (These are usually the underlying reasons for many teenage girls deliberately setting out to become pregnant.) Steve did not want to know about the baby and ended the relationship; ultimately, Karen's mother became the other person most involved, both in the pregnancy and in the first years of her grandchild's life.

As the pregnancy developed, family circumstances became increasingly difficult. Many adjustments had to be made, and finance was a particular problem. However, the relationship between Karen and her mother improved as the birth became imminent. It is now four years since Karen's daughter was born and, though the going has been tough, she has proved to be a good mother. She is now studying for some qualifications at evening classes and coping with a part-time job while her child attends nursery school.

A teenage pregnancy is inevitably accompanied by sadness over the loss of freedom in one so young and the enormous responsibility that having a baby brings. Pregnancy disrupts education and demands many sacrifices, not just from the young parents but from their parents too. It is a situation that usually brings tension into a household. But it may also bring joy too, as a new family member arrives, who has no idea of his history!

7

Leaving home

Around the end of September, a strange phenomenon takes place on roads leading to colleges and universities. Cars in their hundred groan along the motorways, laden with bicycles, squeaky-clean duvets and numerous bags and boxes suggesting that Mum has yet to be convinced that supermarkets exist near campuses. Somewhere, underneath the cans, biscuits, coffee, kettle and ubiquitous pot-noodle, your teenager is trying to identify which feeling is uppermost – excitement, anticipation or apprehension? He is probably feeling all these and a lot more beside! A significant rite of passage is about to begin – leaving home!

Although only about a third of eighteen-year-olds leave home, the figure gets larger later on in adolescence. Of course, young people move out for a variety of reasons not just to go to college or university: they may be starting a new job, sharing a flat with friends, maybe even getting married.

Attitudes towards leaving home vary from family to family. Some parents accept it as a natural step from adolescence to adulthood. Others can't wait for their offspring to go! However, the majority probably experience a mixture of feelings: sadness that a much-loved child is taking the first adult step of independence; perhaps also a tinge of guilt that they themselves now have the opportunity to enjoy more space, physically and emotionally.

Handling separation

Often parents are 'broken in' gently to the fact that their children will eventually leave them through the short periods of time spent away from home at camps, on school trips or exchange visits. Events like these give both sides the opportunity to familiarise themselves with what separation is going to be like. Loosening the ties financially and allowing children to budget for themselves is also a helpful step in the separation process. This can start early by giving pocket money which then becomes a clothing or personal allowance as the young person gets older. Whatever the method, it should involve a gradual progression, equipping the youngster for responsibility and independence in adulthood.

Leaving home may be more of an emotional wrench for the parent than the child. When our younger daughter left home, I kept the bedroom door open so that I could look in on a continually clean and tidy room! The novelty soon wore off, however, and suddenly it all seemed so unnatural and empty. I was pleased when holidays came around again and the room regained its familiar chaotic, lived-in look!

Other superficial adjustments have to be made too. Mum may continue to use familiar recipes and end up with loads of leftovers in the fridge. There are also the occasions when items such as Marmite, peanut butter and packets of crisps are thrown into the shopping trolley; then you get home and realise that they will probably sit in the cupboard for ages. So much for the little things. Let's move on to the bigger, more significant issues that surround 'leaving home'.

The 'empty nest syndrome'

The 'empty nest syndrome', as it has affectionately become known, is a relatively new concept. Years ago, the family was less mobile and extended families were common: granny would live up the road and uncles, aunts and cousins in adjacent streets. Expectations and roles were much more clearly defined and there were always children around, looked after by a willing grandmother or aunt.

Now society has changed and people tend to move away from their families, and even from the places where they were born. The family unit has changed in structure too, and, when the last child leaves home, parents may feel that a huge gap has opened up in their lives.

Some parents are left grieving over a phase that can never return. If you have spent the parenting years living through your children, you will feel the change even more keenly and will have to find a new means of fulfilment. Teenagers can tell if their parents are dependent on them, and, because life is all ahead for them, may respond with resentment or passive rebellion. If children feel blackmailed into staying near the family home, they may leave emotionally instead of physically: they may stay in the same house or in the same area but become increasingly angry inside, which will bring about an even greater deterioration in the relationship with their parents.

All offspring must leave home emotionally when they do go, though this doesn't mean that love, friendship and respect for their parents are abandoned! Inability to leave emotionally has serious consequences on any marital relationship the young person may eventually have. Many marriages flounder because one side of the partnership is still clinging emotionally to their family, which disrupts the new bond with their husband or wife.

'Leaving home' is a two-way process. As their *raison d'être* departs in a flurry of activity and parents wave goodbye to many years of self-sacrifice and caring, the time comes to evaluate what has changed. This is an opportunity for new beginnings, both individually and as a couple. It is advisable, therefore, to endeavour to pursue your own interests well before this time arrives. If you haven't, don't put it off any longer – get started! Begin by exploring what you want more time to do. Re-train for employment? Pursue an interest? Spend more time with other people? Or get a job in your church or in your community?

As I said at the beginning of this chapter, adolescents leave home for a variety of different reasons and move on to a number of different lifestyles. Let's explore a few of these in more detail.

College or university

The first weeks of adjusting to campus life can prove euphoric for some and a nightmare for others! As you help your son or daughter drag luggage up numerous flights of stairs (why does their room always have to be on the top floor, at the end of a corridor, through swing doors that even Samson would find difficult to push?) you can sense the buzz of excitement and activity. It seems hard to believe that in a short time these strangers who are being eyed with guarded interest may become close friends.

As you drive away, perhaps with the occasional sniff and blink, you are confronted with a space in the car and a silence which is a reflection (if this is the last child to leave) of what awaits you at home. Meanwhile, back at campus, frantic activity will be taking place. Each youngster will be stamping individuality onto his or her bare, impersonal room, and finding out who is creative, who is tidy (it won't last!) and who is going to leave everything to everybody else!

The euphoria quickly evaporates into mundane routine when the first essay deadline looms and the harsh reality of student budgeting becomes apparent. Personally, I think students often get an unfavourable press: the majority are diligent and hardworking, often doing jobs in the evenings and during the holidays to supplement their grants. However, an active social life is also important for students, and it's hard to imagine that the silent figures creeping into the 9 am lecture are the same ones who seem to come alive at 9 pm! Trying to find the right balance between work and play is a delicate occupation, with the scales tipped heavily one way or the other several times a term.

The first weeks may be a time of easy adjustment for many, especially the more gregarious, outgoing types. On the whole, student years give an opportunity to assert independence and forge lasting friendships. For most there are very few problems to be negotiated on the way (like having to break it to Mum and Dad that you are going to your friend's home for the holidays – and hearing the sharp intake of breath on the other end of the phone!).

But there are always those who try to put on a brave face, though they are in fact finding it difficult to adjust to their new sub-culture and environment. College life is definitely the survival of the fittest, and there will inevitably be those who can cope with the academic side, but who struggle with the social. The quiet introvert may find a friend in another introvert, or he may feel quite isolated if he is not confident enough to integrate with others.

College and the Christian

College and university life can be a real culture shock for the teenager with an active Christian faith. While the majority of colleges bend over backwards to be politically correct and not to offend by proffering sexist or racist remarks, they often show no mercy to Christians, and strong faith may be discounted both by fellow students and lecturers as a psychological crutch to support inadequacy. Christian beliefs may also be seriously challenged in an environment where discussion and criticism are par for the course. Perhaps this informs us as churches, with a responsibility for young people, of the importance of a firm foundation and grounding in Christian teaching, and an equipping to think through and give the reasons for our convictions. A flimsy, superficial response without substance will quickly be torn apart.

Christian Unions in colleges and universities really need to build up a vital, committed membership so as to avoid being seen, perhaps unjustly, as a club for wimps who occasionally stick up badly produced posters with obscure questions on them. A good CU is an effective means not only of sharing faith but of providing friendship and support to young Christians. Prayer and encouragement from the home church is also valuable, and a letter from another Christian can be a lifeline in moments of loneliness and isolation.

Drugs

It won't be long before your son or daughter is exposed to the easy availability of drugs on campus, though more than likely they will already have come across these in school or at sixth-form college. (Statistics show that 47% of young people have experimented with drugs before they are even 15.) The majority will decline to get involved, but some may try soft drugs. As a parent, you may equate being exposed to a drug culture with being part of it, but this isn't necessarily so. If your son or daughter is reliably informed about drugs and the effects they have, they will be reasonably well-equipped to deal with any situations that arise.

After I had experienced the bitter-sweetness of reaching forty, I decided to become a full-time student again and obtain my degree. My own children were travelling abroad or just finishing 'A' levels, so I had more time to pursue further study, something I had wanted to do for ages. I got a real insight into student life, and I loved it! Being part of a group of youngsters around the same age as my own children initially made me a little apprehensive – but it wasn't long before I was accepted as one of them, a fellow student. I only felt my age when we were studying the youth culture of the 60s in sociology and I found myself sighing, 'Alas, I remember it well' to the young, extremely trendy lecturer!

I too had my surprise moments, such as the occasion when I was offered cannabis to 'help with revision for the exams'. It was bad enough getting my brain into gear after so many study-free years, without entertaining drugs: they would probably have finished me off!

Money

A real headache for most students is how to stretch the termly grant to last its allocated time. It is all too easy to approach the bank or student loan facility for a 'top up', but this can have the effect of storing up huge commitments for the future. Some graduates find themselves unable to get on top of their debts for years. There seems little parents can do, however, in a situation where students' needs far outweigh their income. Even if parental cash *is* available, it is perhaps unhelpful to bale your offspring out continually and hinder them from ever learning to stand on their own two feet.

The first job

Many youngsters do not opt for further education but choose instead to go straight into a job or career that offers training. Getting a job these days is not the easy option it may once have been. Whether you are qualified or not, there is no guarantee that employment awaits you. Redundancy and joblessness seem to be a fact of life, and we can sympathise with the young person who leaves school or college with every expectation of getting work and is then left frustrated that there is nothing appropriate on offer.

Even getting a job is not necessarily an easier option than going on to further study. For rather than remaining involved with their peer group, your child has to cope with life in an established adult environment, going from being a big fish in a little pond to being a little fish in a big pond that is occasionally frequented by sharks!

Living at home

As a result of the recession of the last few years, increasing numbers of young people are choosing to stay at home because they cannot afford to rent or take on a mortgage, even though they may be working. For parents who find their offspring still living at home, the transition between being at school and having a job may be difficult to manage. In parents' eyes nothing has changed. But their child may feel that, because he is now working, his status within the family unit ought to be raised.

The first anxious moment may be when the new pay cheque arrives. There is an air of expectancy on the part of parents that an agreed amount will be transferred to the family purse to contribute towards household expenses. This seemingly adult transaction can, however, be fraught with embarrassment, resentment or even passive hostility! It may seem that formerly caring, generous souls have suddenly turned grasping and mercenary. However, if your child has stopped being financially dependent, he needs to establish that independence by realistically contributing to the family budget. A direct debit from your offspring's bank account to yours may help to place this new responsibility on a business-like footing. Living at home is, according to what I have gleaned from many parents, a bargain – an outside landlord would be likely to charge much more.

That your child will leave home eventually is inevitable. How this time is negotiated depends on how well you prepare for it beforehand. It is a real joy when youngsters who have left home return to visit Mum and Dad because they want to. There may be a few, however, who find the nest, with all mod cons laid on, far too cosy and convenient. They will need a gentle push or, if this doesn't work, a hearty shove to get them out there into the big wide world.

Flat-sharing

If your child does move out of the family home to share a flat with friends, you may experience the same sense of loss as parents whose children depart for university or college. It is an experience in itself to visit your offspring in their new flat. But please behave and keep any suggestions for improvements to yourself unless asked. They probably love sitting on the floor and eating while watching the box, even if you don't!

Off to see the world

The 'Grand Tour' of the late nineteenth century may have been reserved for the elite and those whose families were particularly well-endowed financially, but today's youngsters have made their own mark upon global travel with the 'not-so-grand tour' – by backpack!

With foreign countries more accessible now, and every corner of the world no more than a few days away, it is an opportunity too good to miss. And what better time than adolescence when schooling ends and the harsh reality of employment, mortgages and family life seems light years away?

Foreign travel certainly sorts out the brave from the faint-hearted. I can remember thinking, 'Why on earth has she gone *there*!' when I had an SOS from our daughter in a remote part of India requesting that I send six pairs of pants out ASAP 'because the rats have chewed them all up'! Whatever the pitfalls, it has to be acknowledged that exploring new cultures and societies, becoming self-reliant and responsible, can only strengthen and build character. There is no end of opportunity these days for young people to go abroad under the auspices of Christian agencies and voluntary schemes which combine teaching and development with work in the local community. Well-established agencies have a high standard of care for those who volunteer, but don't hesitate to check them out. No organisation with any credibility should be surprised at being vetted; in fact they would probably welcome such interest.

Half the appeal of travelling abroad seems to be that you can move on when the mood takes you or stay because the place really exceeds expectations. Whatever the situation, no amount of well-meaning advice seems to prepare loving parents for saying 'Goodbye', knowing that it may be months or even years before they see their offspring again. The following points may serve to help not only you, but your teenager too, if overseas travel is on the agenda in the near future. This is not a comprehensive list – just a few tips not always given in travel books and leaflets.

- It is all too easy to try to organise your children's packing according to your own ideas. The big fluffy towel may seem essential to you, but four tea towels sewn together provides a far more practical alternative – it takes up hardly any room and dries extremely quickly.

- A large packet of multi-vitamins and minerals is a good way of supplementing your offspring's diet. Encourage your child to keep the lid on, though. There is a cockroach somewhere in Asia which is so fortified by now that he has probably bred a hoard of 'superbugs'!

- Check with the organisation or travel company on the kinds of things that are useful to pack in a first aid kit, and don't forget to put in an AIDS pack in case a syringe or needle is required. Other useful items are an inflatable pillow (they will then be able to catch up on sleep almost anywhere), a universal plug for the non-existent bath, a plastic door-wedge to keep unwelcome callers out of their room, and a secure money-belt.

- Family photos are always a good idea to take, both for the traveller and for those whom she meets. In some countries there is an insatiable interest in families, and photos always seem to provide a good talking point.

- Check with travel agents and the foreign office too, about areas in the world where it really would not be safe to travel. Ask your son or daughter to provide you with a general itinerary, and urge them to keep in regular contact by phone (an international phone card such as those from British Telecom would be a good idea) or by letters or postcards.

• Send your own letters in advance to the Poste Restante, where mail can be held until it is collected. Encourage your son or daughter to write about their thoughts and experiences in their letters. It's amazing how difficult it is to recall every memorable moment afterwards.

• Do pray for protection for your child. Many overseas countries are steeped in occult practice and she will not be able to discern every magic artifact or evil presence, so prayer is vital. Pray too that your son or daughter will be safe from any kind of physical harm wherever they are.

Perhaps one of the most difficult aspects of travel to adjust to is returning home. If your son or daughter has spent a considerable time away, this may be quite traumatic. On the one hand, they are looking forward to meeting everyone again; but, on the other, the reorientation process can prove difficult. Seeing such a variety of food in the shops and so much of it may provoke feelings of anger and confusion. Be sensitive about this – it is just as much a culture shock for them returning as it was going.

There is little doubt that when young people leave their own country for a protracted period, they come back changed. Living in a different culture with different values, especially if they have been in places where poverty is rife and possessions extremely basic, has a profound effect and often changes attitude. Whatever the motivation for travelling – to have an enjoyable holiday or to live with people and acquire a greater knowledge of their culture – the result is of lasting value. A more global perspective develops a young character, and often the adolescent who left will return a mature, independent adult.

8

Coping single-handed

If there is any one family group that particularly deserves recognition, it is the single-parent family. It is difficult enough to manage family matters when there are two parents, let alone cope on your own.

The single parent

Some say that being a single parent involves being both Mum and Dad to children, but my interpretation is that it means being 200 per cent Mum *or* Dad, with all of the workload and no one to share it with. The role often stretches you emotionally and physically to the limit, especially when there are few others to provide much in the way of support.

With the divorce rate rising, more families than ever are having to adjust to becoming single-parent households. Sometimes divorced couples maintain a good, co-operative relationship with each other, but in many situations there is tension or a lack of communication that has soured the relationship leaving the child feeling like 'piggy in the middle'. The parent at home may have all kinds of anxieties regarding how their son or daughter gets on with the parent who has left, and this can lead to the child getting the third degree whenever he or she comes home from a visit. This is unhelpful and distressing, especially since children usually feel loyalty towards both parents. Recent legislation is designed to enable conciliation and effective communication between parents, and this will ultimately benefit the children too.

Of course, there are other circumstances that lead to someone coping with children alone. It may be that you never married and have brought your child up single-handed from the beginning. Or you may have experienced bereavement when your children were small. Whatever the situation, single parenthood has its own unique problems.

- The social lives of teenagers can leave those of adults in the shade! Parents may seem to spend all their time either arranging transport or ferrying their offspring back and forth from friends' houses, youth club and the cinema, often late at night and sometimes when they would relish an early night. For the single parent, this can be a real problem, especially if you do have to work and must be up early the next morning.

- Decision-making too can seem an onerous task. There's no one with whom to talk through the different choices and their consequences, and no one to support the decisions you have made. Particularly daunting are those relating to your child's education, as this plays such a big part in shaping and directing his future.

- Although holidays are a welcome break, they can be difficult, especially when the children are out enjoying themselves and the lone parent is left in unfamiliar circumstances on their own. Doubling-up with friends or relatives may be possible and will give you a chance to go off and 'do your own thing' from time to time.

- If you belong to a local church, there are often activities going on which will give both you and your child an opportunity to build friendships. And churches, *please* be sensitive to those who can't come out for midweek events without a sitter for the under-15s. Away-days and church holidays are good opportunities for single parents to feel part of a larger family, so always provide the means to make it possible – tickets and perhaps an invitation to go with another family in the church as guests if necessary. This way churches can truly be one family without any particular unit feeling inferior.

Bringing up children on your own is hard work, so if you are a single parent, grab every offer of support with both hands – help with transport or an opportunity for an evening out. There is no point in letting pride or an inappropriate spirit of independence sabotage what could make your life easier. Take every opportunity that comes to enrich a time when you will need all the reassurance and support you can get.

'Lost' adolescence

The majority of teenagers see adolescence as a time when they can taste freedom, spread their wings a little, take more responsibility for themselves and loosen family ties. There are, however, quite a significant number of youngsters who never have this freedom because of duties and responsibilities at home. Although this chapter has been primarily about the parent going it alone, it is worth exploring the experience of the child who has to cope single-handed.

'Lost' adolescence may occur because a parent is disabled in some way or has severe emotional problems, and they become over-dependent on their offspring. The child finds himself in a role-reversal situation, where he must prematurely take on the role of chief carer and the responsibility for making decisions that may be inappropriate at his stage of development. A youngster in such a situation may feel that to leave home would be to 'abandon' Mum or Dad. His chances of going to college may be affected or, less significantly, his opportunity to enjoy day-to-day activities, or go away for the occasional break, is limited.

There are other kinds of parent who put an enormous burden upon their children, such as the parent who has a problem with alcohol abuse. The constant round of taking charge, putting the drunken parent to bed and searching for hidden bottles can catapult the young person into a very frustrated adulthood all too soon. There is, thankfully, practical support from agencies like Al Anon for youngsters in this kind of situation. However, the emotional tensions, which are all too easily suppressed due to practical demands, do not emerge until later in life. The adult may harbour resentment about his 'lost' adolescence, and attempt to return to it in ways that are inappropriate at this latter stage in his life.

If as a lone parent you are aware that your dependence on your teenager is greater than that of other parents, do ensure that your child has ample opportunity to socialise with her own age group and encourage her to do so. Perhaps you could also explore if help might be available from any other source, either within the family or outside it.

The practical problems of single parenthood may *seem* peripheral to the more heavy, emotional ones, but they are very much part of the ongoing responsibility of the lone parent and can take their toll. It is important to identify your own needs as a single parent. There may be things that you would like to share with someone who doesn't know you or your situation and who could offer an objective viewpoint. Counselling can be beneficial and may give you the personal space you need to address any negative feelings you may have, such as anger and rejection, which often accompany a breakdown in a relationship. Counselling could also help affirm you in your role as a parent and build up the skills you have gained through having to use your own resources and coping alone. It is so important that you give time to your own personal development as well as that of your child.

The death of a parent

Experiencing the death of a parent in adolescence is a cruel blow. With all the emotional confusion of growing up, being faced with such a loss at this time is traumatic. Others may perceive the bereaved husband or wife as needing the most support, and may expect that they, in turn, will help their children cope with grief. However, this may not be the case. Teenagers can 'fall through the net' and be unable to grieve properly for the parent they have lost. As churches, we should be aware of this and ensure that someone is available to youngsters until their bereaved parent can take over again. At this time in their life, young people often have a heavy workload, what with homework, school projects and exams – and their work cannot but be affected. Schools have student counsellors and other people trained in pastoral care. If you are a bereaved parent, do try to use these resources, or engage the help of an adult whom your child trusts and can talk to freely.

During the ensuing weeks, months and even years, the bereaved family will gradually evolve a new pattern of life. Your son or daughter will get used to having only one parent around, and you will be a vital source of security. As time moves on, however, especially if the lost parent is not easily talked about, difficulties may arise that add to the usual problems of the teenage years.

When a child thinks of the parent who has died, he will remember what he or she was like at the time of death, and may come to have a slightly unreal, idealised image. Positive aspects of the lost parent's personality will almost certainly become amplified, while negative ones will lessen and diminish. Memories may be highly selective, and a rosy view will gloss over inadequacies and failings. Any attempt by the living parent to redress the balance by gently pointing out less positive characteristics is likely to result in accusations of disloyalty.

The bereaved parent may not find it easy to integrate all the aspects of the dead loved one in order to grieve for the real, more whole person; a child may find it much harder. It is now widely accepted that a young person may take much longer to get over a close bereavement than was previously thought. The pedestal on which the youngster places the dead parent has the effect of keeping him or her remote and out of reach. This pedestal has to come down in order for the memory to become accessible and the child to go through the grieving process properly. Initially this can be hard to do. For the living parent, exercising discipline over a teenager with no back up or support can be soul-destroying if he or she is constantly being compared with someone who could do no wrong!

If you are bereaved, try to share your feelings of loss with your children. One teenager whose father died remained angry with his mother for years, but did not admit it either to her or to himself until much later in his life. In the weeks and months after his father's death he never saw his mother cry. He assumed that this was because she didn't feel sad about his father's death and hadn't loved him very much. What actually happened was that his mother cried alone, at night, when all her grief came flooding out. She didn't want to distress her son further by crying in front of him, and was convinced that she was caring for him by keeping her feelings bottled up like this.

Years later, when mother and son talked about this period of their lives, it released a tension that had lain between them. They were finally able to share their thoughts and tears together and to heal their relationship.

Divorce

A marriage may cease, but you and your ex both remain your children's parents until you die. Your relationship continues even though it may change in order to be effective in the new circumstances. It is vital, even if the divorce has been less than amicable, (is there *ever* a really amicable divorce?) for both sides to retain their dignity and to value the redeemable parts of the marriage. If your son or daughter only hears the other parent being blamed and slighted, they will be unable to form a relationship with that parent based on their own perceptions. There has to be an integration of both the good and bad parts of a person for a relationship to develop. However bad your marriage was, your child may have experienced the parenting as adequate. Don't tear down or devalue the good memories that remain.

As we have seen in bereavement and, indeed, in step-parenting, when there is a divorce a child may gain an idealised view of one parent and an unfairly negative view of the other. The teenager's regard for the absent parent may increase because he is lavished with expensive presents or exciting holidays whenever he goes for a visit. The parent who stayed, on the other hand, has to cope with the everyday caring with all its ordinariness and mundane routine, often on a tight budget.

The child may also direct his anger about the divorce at the parent who stayed. This parent may feel the sting of unsaid remarks such as 'If you had been a better wife/husband, Mum/Dad would never have left!' With such feelings around, sometimes verbally expressed, at other times held back in passive hostility, it is small wonder that many lone parents feel they are in a 'no win' situation and almost give up trying to get anything right. 'In adolescence a mother's place is in the wrong!' This saying by the psychologist Winnicot is certainly tried and tested!

Perhaps one of the most helpful ways for a child to establish a good relationship with both Mum *and* Dad, even when they don't live together or have a positive relationship, is through both parents emphasising the *differences* in circumstances and character rather than the good or bad. Negotiating and sharing the responsibilities between you and your child's other parent, and establishing some mutually agreed ground rules, will help your teenager to have as normal and as stable a life as can be expected under the circumstances. Taking such steps will prevent one parent playing the child off against the other, and provide some form of security and cohesion. With so many of their peer group likely to be in similar families, the stigma of being odd or different has now gone. But the need for sensitive handling of the situation still remains.

9

Living together or marriage?

Fourteen out of every twenty couples who get married today have lived together first, and the number is rising. In the 1960s fewer than one in twenty couples lived together before marriage,. Confronting these hard facts is saddening for Christians, especially when it appears that couples who live together before they marry are 50% more likely to divorce within five years.

Christian parents should not imagine that they are somehow exempt from this trend in society. I know many whose offspring have chosen to live together with their boy/girlfriend. Their parents have had to come to terms with a way of life that does not fit with their faith. I would like to take a closer look at both cohabitation and marriage and see how they affect the couples who choose them. It may be useful, too, to 'unpack' some of the myths and prejudices put forward to champion each of these situations, so as to bring expectations into line with reality.

The Christian response

First, let's look at your response as Christian parents when your adolescent announces that he is moving in with his girlfriend and they intend to live together. You may already have been aware that they have been sleeping together, but now they are 'going public'. Along with your natural concern, you will probably, inevitably, be caught up in all sorts of anxieties. (We've visited these a number of times now!) 'What will our friends say?' 'How will the fellowship or congregation react?' 'Will *we* be judged by people?' Of course, other Christians will make their own value judgements, and there may well be the occasional barbed comment. Ultimately, however, you will discover who your real friends are – those who value you for the person *you* are and who don't hold you responsible for your adult children's behaviour. These are the friends with whom you can talk through your feelings.

Nevertheless, coming to terms with a situation that you don't agree with is difficult. On the one hand, you don't want to seem hypocritical in condoning something that is not compatible with your beliefs. On the other, you don't wish to alienate your child and spoil the relationship you have with him. How can the situation be managed effectively?

I have known parents who have taken a punitive line and refused to visit the couple in their new home. Perhaps we can understand their reasons, but what is there to gain by this course of action? You stand to lose a loving relationship with both your offspring and his partner. A more positive, constructive approach would be to share your convictions in a loving and sensitive way, but to hand the responsibility for their decision over to them. Make it clear, however, that you accept whatever they decide. After all, it is their decision as adults.

If the relationship is a long-term one, it may raise practical issues. Where do they sleep when they come to stay with you? These details will need to be discussed with your child to avoid assumptions being made. You may find that your son is aware of your feelings and respects you too much to cause any embarrassment.

Reasons for living together

With so many youngsters experiencing marital breakdown, whether that of their parents or of other significant relatives, they will naturally be hesitant about making a legal commitment to someone, and may think that if they don't get married in the first place, they will avoid the acrimony and pain of divorce.

I'm sure that we can all empathise with such feelings, but there seems to be an underlying assumption that a long-term relationship can end without pain. Whenever there is loss, there is bound to be grief. There are very few relationships which, when they don't work out, allow either party to walk away with no harm done. Indeed, this does happen, it reduces those involved to disposable assets, to be discarded when they have served their purpose or when something better turns up! It is almost impossible to achieve closeness, security and trust in a relationship that has an optional 'get out' clause, especially when current statistics show that the average length for a 'live in' relationship is approximately two years.

Other reasons for people living together may be largely economic. Two people sharing the rent is a much more viable option than renting two flats separately! Weddings are expensive and many couples decide to live together first and save up to pay for the wedding later.

Social factors may play a part in the decision to live together. Young women may feel vulnerable in large cities and think that moving in with their boyfriend offers a more secure arrangement. And sadly, two people of the same sex living together often gives rise to the automatic assumption that they are a gay couple, and this may make moving in with a person of the opposite sex a more attractive alternative. Sharing a house with several others can help avoid speculation. It is a sad thing that society now appears to set the rules, but Christians need to be aware that this is so, even if we don't agree.

Myths of living together

Let's dispel the myth that living together is a kind of trial marriage, a run through to test out compatibility. In reality, a couple living together are only practising living together! Marriage is built on a completely different set of values. It may be argued that seeing each other every day and night, and accommodating the less romantic aspects of sharing a life, is a way of testing out whether or not you can tolerate each other under stress. Sadly, some *marriages* are embarked upon with the idea that 'if it doesn't work we can split up'. But within a marriage there is far more incentive and commitment to work through individual differences than to accumulate enough reasons to justify your ending the relationship.

Another perception that I have concerning young co-habitees is that they tend to hold back from complete commitment to each other, seeing themselves rather as two individuals who split their finances down the middle and live their own lives. They do not embrace the 'what is mine is yours and what is yours is mine' philosophy of a good marriage. It doesn't follow, however, that by marrying you lose your individuality and identity. Far from it. There may not be such an emphasis on 'even shares' financially, but that is because the whole is seen as having far more value than the sum of the individual parts!

I am not suggesting that young people get married *just* so that they can live together or to please others including their parents. (I have seen disastrous results when this happens.) I *am* suggesting that they consider the advantages and lasting rewards of waiting for the right person. Then, as the relationship progresses, they can think seriously about where it is going, rather than simply jog along, doing everything in the 'wrong' order.

After the 'falling in love' stage has developed into the deeper and more realistic '*being* in love', you usually know whether the relationship is the one for you or not. Falling in love is an idealistic state, highly pleasurable (and we have all been there, at least once!) but also extremely unreliable: everything tends to be seen through rose-coloured specs! It is strongly advisable not to make long-term decisions while in this ecstatic frame of mind. We often see the results of doing this in the media: 'Golden couple swear undying love for each other. This is it for keeps, they say'; then, a year or two later the divorce is announced. When, over a period of time, a love develops that accepts the faults and shortcomings of the other, it is likely that the decision to share life together is based on a far more reliable foundation. Mind you, rose-tinted specs are not unknown in marriage either: many couples assume that any faults in their partners will be magically transformed the minute they tie the knot. Sorry, not so!

So living together is not a substitute for marriage but an alternative choice: the longer a couple live together, the weaker the incentive to marry becomes. There is always something else that has greater claims on their time and on their finances. Marriage, Christians believe, can provide the right basis for family life, freedom for individual personal development and security. It is more than the much maligned 'bit of paper'. It is a public declaration of lifetime commitment to each other within a legal framework that protects, secures and acknowledges this intention. Marriage is a commitment to work through any difficulties together, bring about change and come out the other end with a more rewarding relationship, enriched by a deeper understanding and a greater love for each other.

Finding your partner

Finding a partner who shares the same Christian faith is easier said than done! I have known couples who have married because they were Christians but had little else in common, and it is no wonder that these marriages lack any shared interest or vitality. A shared faith is an important factor but it is not the only one.

Unfortunately, there are churches which push young people into early marriages because they 'feel it to be right' or that 'the Lord has confirmed it'. Some church leaders have pressurised young people to marry so that they can have 'legal' sex, only to find years later that the marriage has dissolved because the foundation was so flimsy. Do beware of people, however spiritual, who seem to know more than you do about whether or not you should marry. The Lord is quite capable of dealing with you directly!

For the Christian, therefore, finding a partner may be quite difficult, and some remain single through choice rather than form relationships with those who do not share their beliefs as well as return their love. 'Where can I find a Christian boy/girlfriend?' is a question young Christians often ask, and there are no easy answers. I would, however, encourage anyone who expects the ideal partner to arrive gift-wrapped on their church doorstep to widen their horizons. Establishing friendships and a social life is valuable for everyone, but even more so for adolescents. There are ample opportunities to meet other young people while involved in voluntary work or overseas aid schemes, at annual Christian events like Soul Survivor and Greenbelt, or on holidays organised for the whole church family.

Waiting

There are those who do marry, and for the Christian couple who have decided to delay sex until after marriage there is the bonus of physical union coming when many other aspects of their relationship have already been established. They have got to know the other person, to trust and respect them. Natural passion and desire for each other can now take their rightful place, and the couple can enjoy each other's bodies to the full, with great pleasure!

Waiting is not easy, however, and I would encourage

church leaders to support couples through marriage preparation groups and to explore the issues arising from the choice to remain celibate until after marriage. Marriage preparation is invaluable for enabling a couple to explore together what they expect from their marriage, how their observations of marriage and their family background will affect what each brings into the relationship and, above all, to build up their communication skills. Marriage preparation can also open up areas which may not have seemed important to the couple who still have an idealistic picture of their future life together. These classes should not consist merely of a 'talk' by a well-meaning vicar; courses should be properly thought through and organised. There is good material available – do use it, or encourage couples to attend weekend groups or courses run by a variety of other organisations.

There are people such as those who would not agree with abstaining from intercourse before marriage, who assume that if you choose to wait you can't have a very healthy sex-drive or that your partner does not turn you on! On the contrary! Celibacy means that control is being exercised and channelled, not necessarily repressed, and the waiting makes sexual activity more exciting when it finally does arrive. This is something that cannot be easily understood if sex is merely the 'night-cap' at the end of a date.

Rachel was the only virgin amongst her friends. When she got engaged, she was very much ridiculed when she told them that she and David were not sexually active. After her marriage, she shared with her friends how wonderful and satisfying sex was. One by one, they admitted their envy and their regret that it would never be like that for them. It is sad if there is nothing new to discover physically with your husband or wife, and sex together is only a re-run of previous relationships.

Early marriage

Because living together is not an option for Christian couples, they may choose to marry at an earlier age than their peers. This brings its own set of problems, not just for the couple themselves but for those around them. There are myths here too that perhaps need to be explored.

The first is that the couple are too young to make any major decisions. If they are under 20, they may not yet be fully developed emotionally. Then again, people do mature differently according to individual personalities and cultures. When you consider that statistics show second and subsequent marriages have a much higher failure rate, this particular argument is flawed.

Another myth of early marriages is that the couple are marrying in haste without giving proper consideration to the responsibilities which marriage entails. If, as should be the case, the pair have gone through many weeks of marriage preparation beforehand, they should have had lots of opportunity to explore together what they expect of their marriage and to discover each other's feelings and anxieties, the issues that make them happy and any fears they have.

In young marriages, perhaps more than most, the couple may find it quite difficult to separate the values and traditions of their own marriage from those of their parents. Many a young couple has had rows over the way to do this or that, each assuming that the way they have always been familiar with is best! It takes maturity and a willingness to change, to evolve a set of values which is of your own making and not the legacy of your parents. Parents must allow some distance to grow between themselves and their young married offspring. They need time to establish their own marriage, and it can be quite intrusive if Mum or Dad keep popping around when they need space to be on their own. Wait to be invited: this is not being formal, merely polite, and will help establish a healthy 'in laws' relationship.

And finally...

Do accept that the standards of your married offspring are their own, not yours. They may be affectionately bonded to that fluff collecting in a corner of their home, so please don't attempt to remove it! The particular lifestyle your children choose to pursue may not conform to what you would have wished for them. Nevertheless, the love and respect you have for each other should overcome any difficulties. Working at your relationship and simply enjoying their company, whatever they are like, will lead to the development of a bond which is rewarding to everyone.

10

Afterthoughts

You probably bought this book because you are (a) about to embark upon the new role of parenting a teenager; or (b) firmly established in the experience and need all the help you can get! I hope that you have acquired some coping mechanisms to sustain you through the sometimes calm, sometimes turbulent waters of adolescence. I also hope that you have retained your humour and your self-esteem!

As one who has 'gone through' this particular rite of passage, I can only encourage you to hang on in there – it is an investment that will reap benefits for both you and your offspring for the rest of your lives. You will gain insight into your own role of parent. And you will find that, at the end of it all, you have a new and rewarding relationship with your child – adult with adult instead of adult with child. After what seems like an interminable length of time, when you feel you have been stretched to your limits, adolescence does actually end quite quickly. One day you will realise just how much you love and respect the new adult who has emerged. You will be delighted to find you can share a meal together or relax in each other's company simply because you both *want* to!

When two people receive that God-given gift of a baby bundled up in innocence, perhaps they don't realise the complex package they are holding. But, however difficult, self-sufficient and argumentative your child becomes, never forget that original vulnerability which is still present and which can be damaged so easily.

Take care of your children's adolescence – you are equipping them to become the honourable adults of the future. When the going gets tough, take comfort in reminding yourself that your adolescents may have adolescents of their own one day! And don't forget – *never* say 'I told you so!' No matter how many times you think it, with a wry smile!

OTHER TITLES FROM
SCRIPTURE UNION

What About It?
Lance Pierson
For 11-14s, this lively book answers questions on topics like God, prayer, faith, sex, relationships, money, drugs, evil and what happens after we die. An in-depth look at the things which puzzle young people as they work through their faith today.

Rap, Rhyme & Reason
Anita Haigh
A vibrant collection of monologues, poems, sketches and raps based on Jesus' life and teaching as depicted in the Gospels. Young people are encouraged to reflect on key issues such as justice, forgiveness, anger, fear and faith. For use in a variety of settings including schools, youth groups, family services and holiday clubs.

The Adventure Begins: A practical guide to exploring the Bible with under-12s
Terry Clutterham
This inspiring book gives practical help on overcoming the difficulties children have with reading the Bible. Offers new insights into how parents and carers can help them engage with the text in a meaningful way.

Scrap Happy
Joan King & Footprints Theatre Co
A five-session resource for people of all ages, designed to build cross-generational friendships. The programme centres around the Scrap Family and can be used with *Scrap Happy – The Video*.

Just Parenting
Christine Wright

For people awaiting the birth of a child or with under 5s, this book is a practical and humorous look at the skills and responsibilities involved in parenting.

Dear God, Can You Wink?
Gillian Raymond

This parental guide to prayer shows how to encourage children to spend time with God. It covers getting to know God, building that relationship, and growing up. Ideas and activities offer practical help in developing a child's prayer life.

'If a book review could contain only one sentence, I would say about this book, "I loved it".' (*Children's Ministry*)

And All the Children said Amen
Ian Knox

Does your family pray together? Do you wish you did? Here is practical advice on all aspects of praying together at home.

'Full of wisdom, reader friendly and a worthwhile addition to any Christian family bookshelf.' (*Parentwise*)

The Bumper Book of Family Activities
John Marshall

Family at home, extended family, church family – we're all in families! This is a collection of activities and games for families of all ages and sizes to celebrate family life.

Family Activity Box
Sue Clutterham

For families who want to study the Bible together, the box contains 100 cards each with a game, 'talkabout', puzzle or activity which leads on to reading the Bible, learning and having fun together at the same time.

How to Stay Sane When Your Family's Cracking Up
Colin Piper, Chris Curtis & Tim Dobson
Steve's mum finds a picture of a woman in his dad's wallet –
and it's not her. Coping with cracking or crumbling family
life, especially for young people

Moving On
Jo Bailey
A lively full-colour booklet answering questions for children
who are moving on to secondary school. It covers everything
from homework to making new friends.

The Schools Work Handbook: Serving God in your Local School
Emlyn Williams
A practical guide for anyone who wants to serve God in
schools, and to help those already involved to develop their
ministry.

Reaching Children
Paul Butler
A look at the difficulties, the challenges and the excitement
of making Jesus known to children, with help on understanding the child's world and presenting the gospel.
    'Heartily recommended.' *(Aware)*

Reaching Families
Paul Butler
Statistics show that the family today is facing many changes
and pressures, yet family is God's idea and intention. How
can the people of God reflect the family nature of God in
their life together and in the community around them? This
book considers ways in which churches can reach out to
families and to people living alone with the good news of
Jesus Christ.

Children on the Edge
Christine Leonard

Nine stories show how children live in developing countries. Based on facts from Tear Fund, the fictitious stories give a real insight into other ways of life – from everyday things through to relief agency work in times of disaster.

It makes sense
Stephen Gaukroger

A popular, humorous and compelling look at the reasons why it does make sense to be a Christian. Common arguments against faith are dismantled kindly but firmly.

'This is the book to shove into someone's hand the second they become a Christian.' (*Alpha*)

Desert Depths
Simon Parke

Jim, Tracey and Denis come to the desert in search of 'something'. This is Denis' account of their pilgrimage – one that challenges us to think about our own attitudes to God, to our faith and to other people.

Closer to God: Practical help on your spiritual journey
Ian Bunting (Editor)

We are all on a journey through life, with God. For many it is a struggle. What may help us? In this book members of the Grove Spirituality Group write from personal experience and from their understanding of the way Christians have come closer to God down the centuries.

How to pray when life hurts
Roy Lawrence

Prayer makes a difference because God makes a difference. Where can we find help when a situation seems beyond hope? When a marriage is on the point of breakdown, a disease is diagnosed as incurable, or an addiction is running out of control? Nothing is beyond the reach of Christ. Nothing is beyond the healing difference he can make. Whether we feel guilty or angry, fearful or under pressure, this book offers practical help on *how* to pray when life hurts.

Storytellers: Jesus through the eyes of those who knew him
Andrew Brandon
On the way home from sentencing Jesus to death, Pilate puts a phone call through to his wife... Dai and his wife own a small hotel in the village. Nothing out of the ordinary ever happens until a certain couple come to stay... They call him Digit the Midget, the dwarf with the pocket calculator brain, but after Jesus comes to dinner, Zacchaeus no longer feels like a zero...

Key events and characters of the New Testament are presented with startling freshness in this collection of monologues – 'an unusual and rewarding aid to personal devotion'.